D1407103

'This is sublime   ....ertaining and socially
relevant than most … cricket books.'

Bruce Elder, *Sydney Morning Herald*

'…few books have touched me so deeply. And I expect that *First Tests* would
strike a chord with many others too. The book can be read as an elegy to a
certain sort of Australian childhood – to a way of life – that is now close to
extinct.'

Roy Williams, *Weekend Australian*

'The strength of *First Tests* lies in how it draws continuities across different
eras and celebrates the triumphs of those who developed unorthodox techniques outside the confines of coaching.'

Daniel Herborn, *Sun Herald*

'This is a delightful read, and not just for cricket tragics.'

Rod Moran, *West Australian*

'…Steve Cannane mounts a convincing argument that the backyard game is
the reason for Australia's recent dominance of Test cricket.'

The Age

'It makes for fascinating reading to learn just how dedicated the eventual
Test stars of tomorrow were in their childhood.'

Stuart Wark, cricketweb.net

'Cannane has captured [the] evolution of the Australian cricketer with a
mixture of humour and nostalgia.'

Suresh Menon, *allsports magazine*

First Tests

Great Australian Cricketers
and the Backyards that Made Them

STEVE CANNANE

ABC
Books

The ABC 'Wave' device is a trademark of the
Australian Broadcasting Corporation and is used
under licence by HarperCollins*Publishers*Australia.

First published in Australia in 2009
This edition published in 2010
by HarperCollins*Publishers*Australia Pty Limited
ABN 36 009 913 517
harpercollins.com.au

HarperCollins*Publishers*
Level 13, 201 Elizabeth Street, Sydney, NSW 2000, Australia
31 View Road, Glenfield, Auckland 0627, New Zealand
A 53, Sector 57, Noida, UP, India
77–85 Fulham Palace Road, London, W6 8JB, United Kingdom
2 Bloor Street East, 20th floor, Toronto, Ontario M4W 1A8, Canada
10 East 53rd Street, New York NY 10022, USA

National Library of Australia Cataloguing-in-Publication data:

Cannane, Steve.
    First tests : great Australian cricketers and the backyards
    that made them / Steve Cannane.
    2nd ed.
    ISBN: 978 0 7333 2906 7
    Cricket grounds – Australia.
    Cricket players – Australia.
    Cricket – Australia – History.
796.358068

Cover design by Christa Moffitt, Christabella Designs, adapted by Alicia Freile
Cover image from Pictures Collection, State Library of Victoria
*Lane next to Harvey home [where Neil and his brothers learned to play cricket] Shows Harvey
batting with some local boys in the laneway next to his family home, ca. 1948-55*
Internal design and layout by Agave Creative Group
Printed and bound in Australia by Griffin Press
70gsm Classic used by HarperCollins*Publishers* is a natural, recyclable product made
from wood grown in sustainable forests. The manufacturing processes conform to the
environmental regulations in the country of origin, Finland.

Dedicated to the memory of my father
Tom Cannane, who learnt to play cricket
with a hunk of wood on a dairy farm in Coraki
and taught me how to play in the backyard.

Contents

The Originals – Self-made men from Trumper to Bradman

The Hard Road – Depression-era kids and the rise of street cricket

The Radio Age – Synthetic Tests make backyard Tests more authentic

Suburban Sprawl – The post-war building boom creates a nation of cricket pitches

The TV Age – watching Tests, playing Tests and imitating your heroes

Introduction

WHEN AUSTRALIA CAME to dominate world cricket in the 1990s, much was made of the role of the Australian Cricket Academy. Nations who'd copped a hiding from Australia sent delegations to Adelaide to discover the secrets behind the facilities and training methods that produced the likes of Adam Gilchrist, Ricky Ponting and Glenn McGrath. Copycat cricket academies soon sprang up in other parts of the world and Australian coaches became exportable commodities.

But was poaching coaches and checking out the Academy nets really the best approach to mimicking the Australian way? Australia dominated world cricket for sustained periods before the Academy existed. As of April 2010, Australia had won 47.01 per cent of the Tests they'd played in more than 130 years of competition. England rated next best with 34.89 per cent. Clearly, the reasons for Australia's long-run cricketing dominance go deeper than an elite training facility set up in 1987.

Those visiting delegations of cricket officials might have been better off hanging out around old sheds, Hills Hoists and suburban driveways. The backyard has been the real academy of cricket in Australia. It's there, and in the streets and local parks, that Australia's best cricketers honed their skills and their competitive instincts.

They learned how to avoid a hard ball fired in at their head by older brothers keen to bat. How to hit the ball along the ground to avoid the 'six and out' rule. They found a way to adapt to sub-standard pitches, ball tampering and dodgy umpiring. It was here that they hit, bowled and fielded enough balls to give them a chance of competing at the elite level. The much-hyped Academy, now called the Centre for Excellence, has been a decent finishing school. But it's the Australian backyards, the open space and fair weather, that have given Australia its real competitive advantage.

Test cricketers don't make it to the top on talent alone. They have to put in thousands of hours of practice from childhood to adulthood. Malcolm Gladwell in his book *Outliers: The Story of Success* makes a compelling case that success in sport, music and other fields comes not from innate talent, but from hard work. Gladwell argues to reach the top you need to practise your craft in the formative years for around ten thousand hours. As neuroscientist Daniel Levitin says, 'It seems that it takes the brain this long to assimilate all that it needs to know to achieve true mastery.'

Ten thousand hours is a huge amount of time. Not everyone has the time or facilities to practise this obsessively. But in Australia, the backyard has provided the opportunity for budding Test cricketers to put in their ten thousand hours. As Martin Chappell, father of three Test cricketers, said, 'I spent 22 years in club cricket, but I would say that by the time each one of the boys was 14 he had faced more deliveries than I had in my whole career.' The Chappell brothers started facing up to a hard ball in the backyard at the age of two. They had a decent-sized yard and a hunger for competitive play. Once they got home from school there was no waiting around for Mum or Dad to drive them to practice. They could throw their school bags in the house and get on with it.

Of course it's not just how often you practise, it's how you practise. Many of the players in this book came up with highly efficient ways of maximising the value of their practice time. By hitting a golf ball up against a tank stand, Don Bradman faced more balls per hour than he would playing down the park. Keith Miller and Betty Wilson perfected their strokes by repetitively hitting a ball in a stocking hanging from the clothesline, adjusting the height to replicate different kinds of deliveries. Clarrie Grimmett trained his dog to fetch cricket balls on his backyard pitch, so he could spend less time retrieving and more time bowling.

All of these players took their backyard games very seriously. They weren't just hitting balls. In their minds they were playing real Test matches. Some games were played with more spirit than an Ashes decider. Sid Barnes carried a scar for life on his upper lip after he was 'shanghaied' by a neighbourhood rival over an umpiring decision. Mike and David Hussey's backyard games would invariably end with Dave locking himself in the family car after a punch-up. Trevor Chappell chased his brother Greg down the street with an axe after one of their backyard Tests turned ugly. As Greg Chappell once said, 'The toughest cricket I played was in the backyard against my older brother. After playing in the backyard against Ian, Test cricket was a breeze.'

More often than not, Australia's great cricketers had access to open spaces, either in the backyard or close to home. Richie Benaud practised on the back verandah. Bill O'Reilly learned how to bowl his wrong 'un against a gatepost. Adam Gilchrist had a net set up in his backyard. Bob Simpson played against his brothers on a disused tennis court 50 yards down the road. Glenn

McGrath bowled ball after ball at a 44-gallon drum behind a machinery shed on the family farm. Ian Healy played in school nets across the road from his house.

The backyards and streets they played in had a huge influence on the way they played their cricket. Don Bradman's unique grip, stance and backlift all evolved in response to the pace at which the golf ball rebounded off the tank stand. Greg Chappell's trademark flick off the hip came about because the leg side of his backyard wicket offered the best scoring opportunities. Alan Davidson bowled accurately because he had to. If he missed the stumps on his home-made pitch, he had to chase the ball down the hill into the scrub. Doug Walters played spin with ease because his ant-bed backyard pitch spun viciously. Neil Harvey's immaculate footwork came from playing balls darting off cobblestones.

Few of these players were raised in privileged families. Arthur Mailey was born in a slum. Sid Barnes and Ray Lindwall lost parents at a young age. Two of Victor Trumper's siblings died of tuberculosis. Neil Harvey grew up in impoverished Fitzroy during the Depression. As a teenager, Glenn McGrath did back-breaking work to help make the family farm viable. Dennis Lillee lived in a Housing Commission area of Perth. All of them had a hunger to win, a desire to make it to the top, and an ability to adapt to tough conditions. Most of them went to state schools or grew up in country areas. Rarely were they the kids who had access to all the best equipment and the truest pitches. Charlie Macartney batted on dirt pitches and wooden wharves. Dennis Lillee bowled on a lino pitch with sandy footholds. Neil Harvey battled away on the cobblestones. Bill O'Reilly bowled with a chiselled down banksia tree-root.

But the advantages they did have – warm weather and open spaces – were maximised. The backyard, the typical environment for unstructured play in Australia, provides an efficient and competitive environment for cricket. The backyard fence and the 'six and out' rule means you're not chasing leather, (or fur, or banksia roots) all day. Usually somewhere between one and five are playing. It's not like street cricket in India or beach cricket in the West Indies, where you might have to wait a while to get a bat or bowl. Each player is in the game and using their skills at all times. Most of the time you're playing your siblings. That ensures it's a fight to the death. Parents played a big role too. Adam Gilchrist's father Stan built an astroturf pitch and installed a bowling machine in their backyard. Victor Trumper's father Charles would throw balls at him for two hours every morning before school. Doug Walters' parents would play Test matches with the kids in between milking the cows. Brett Lee's dad Bob would take him and his brothers down to the nets after he knocked off from work at the local steelworks. Lou Benaud, taught his five-year-old son Richie how to bat by clearing out a school store room and getting him to hit balls against the wall.

All of the cricketers I spoke to thought their formative experiences in the backyard were critical in shaping them as cricketers. Of course, playing backyard cricket repetitively won't help a talentless cricketer play for his country. Nor is backyard cricket the sole secret to Australian success. As former Australian captain and coach Bob Simpson puts it, 'We are the best organised cricket country in the world even down to the junior levels and we always have been.'

This organisational structure allows players with talent and persistence to work their way up through the grades, being exposed to tougher and more talented players as they climb each rung. The cricket structure helps too. A high proportion of cricket in Australia is played over two days, with around

80 overs bowled per innings. Batsmen learn how to build an innings, to bat for a day and score centuries. Bowlers become familiar with spending a day in the field, striving to take a wicket in hot conditions in their third or fourth spell. English cricket with its emphasis on one-day matches and declaration games provides less of these opportunities, and its cricketers aren't as well-rounded as a result.

But while the organisational structure of Australian cricket remains strong, the backyard pitches are disappearing. In our capital cities big blocks are being battle-axed. McMansions are eating up open space. Back lanes are cordoned off. Backyards are being blitzed. It's hard to get a game of cricket when there's a pergola or a water feature in the way. Combine this with the fact that Australian kids are becoming less likely to spend their leisure time outdoors running around, and suddenly the foundations of Australian cricket aren't looking so flash. It's an opportune time to look back at the role backyard Tests have played in preparing Australian cricketers for the real thing. Perhaps with the decline in unstructured play and the demise of the suburban backyard, we're witnessing the beginning of the end of Australia's cricket dominance.

The Originals —
Self-made men
from Trumper
to Bradman

THE EARLY GREATS of Australian cricket were products of their time. The period spanning Victor Trumper's early cricket playing days (1880/1890s) to Don Bradman's (1910/1920s) was an era of self-sufficiency. Young men learned how to hunt and farm, how to build things and repair them and how to be creative with limited resources. And so it was with cricket. With restricted access to equipment and coaching, the best cricketers of these generations developed their own way of doing their best with the little they had.

For city kids like Trumper and Arthur Mailey conditions were cramped. Streets, parks, schoolyards, living rooms, even the local bottle works became their playgrounds. Country boys like Bradman and Bill O'Reilly had primitive equipment, but more space and more freedom. Unorthodox but effective methods of batting and bowling were allowed to evolve away from the prying eyes of city coaches.

All of them practised like maniacs. Charlie Macartney hit cricket balls early and often. Clarrie Grimmett built a backyard pitch, trained a fox-terrier to fetch, and became a deadly accurate leg-spin bowler. O'Reilly perfected his wrong 'un against a gatepost. Bradman developed his unique batting style by belting a golf ball against a tank stand.

Victor Trumper

PITCH: In the street, asphalt wickets at school, at Moore Park and eventually his own backyard turf wicket in Chatswood.

BAT: Normal bat.

BALL: Compo ball.

PLAYERS: Victor, father Charles, neighbours and schoolmates.

BACKYARD DRILLS: Hitting ball against the wall, rehearsing strokes.

PLAYERS' COMFORT LEVEL: Early days were tough. Surry Hills was an overcrowded disease-ridden slum.

Late nineteenth-century Surry Hills didn't produce too many things of beauty. The inner-city suburb of Sydney was known for its rat plagues, prostitution, gambling dens and industrial waste. The place stank. Primitive sewerage systems, tanneries, soap works and breweries combined to create a noxious stench. But from the muck emerged a batting gem. Victor Trumper was a cricketer of grace, humility and style. Neville Cardus wrote of him, 'The art of Trumper is like the art in a bird's flight, an art that knows not how wonderful it is. Batting was for him a superb dissipation, a spontaneous spreading of fine feathers.'

It's said that Victor Trumper was born on 2 November 1877, though there is no official record of his birth. He was the eldest of eight siblings. The Trumpers lived in Surry Hills between 1883 and 1896. On the surface, it seems strange that Mosman produced Allan Border, while Surry Hills gave us Victor Trumper. It was the kind of place you might expect an unstylish, gritty batsman to emerge from. Larrikin gangs roamed the streets looking for a fight or someone to fleece. Houses were overcrowded, with as many as four families to a home. There was poor drainage and sewerage, and outbreaks of disease. In 1890 tragedy struck the Trumper family. Vic's sisters Louisa and Clarice, and his grandfather Thomas, all died from tuberculosis within a six-month period. Trumper was just 13.

Children growing up in Surry Hills at the time had to deal with death, disease and destitution. Because they didn't have much money, they were always on the look out for cheap forms of entertainment. This generally meant playing sport, getting up to no good, or a bit of both. Victor took the first option. He played cricket in the summer and rugby in the winter. If he couldn't get a game of cricket in the street, or the park, he'd practise in the tight confines of his backyard, hitting a ball up against the wall, or rehearsing his strokes to imaginary deliveries.

Vic's father Charles watched his boy practise in the backyard and soon realised how dedicated he was. He told J.C. Davis in *The Referee* in February 1913 that this passion was evident from the age of nine or ten. 'He would practise assiduously in our backyard for hours every day, and when I saw to what extent he was taken up with the game I decided to encourage him in every possible way I could.' Charles Trumper was a boot clicker, the most highly skilled job in the footwear industry, responsible for cutting the leather to match the design. Shoes weren't the only thing Charles Trumper was adept at shaping. Although not a cricketer of note himself, he would end up playing a significant role in the development of one of cricket's greatest ever batsmen. Each weekday at 6 am Charles took Victor up to Moore Park where they practised batting for two hours. Training ceased when Charles headed off to work, and Victor to school. He probably thought his son would be better off occupied with hitting cricket balls, than getting caught up with the wayward activities of the local larrikin gangs.

These early morning training sessions started to pay dividends. As Charles recalled: 'It was surprising to note the rapid headway he made as a result of the constant practising. Every day I would note some degree of improvement in his skill with the bat and in his style of play, which, needless to say, was a source of much gratification to me.' It's surprising that Charles Trumper was surprised. A daily, two hour, one-on-one training session will improve the skills of any cricketer, especially one with the innate talents of Trumper. He was later known for his ability to play a range of strokes around the wicket. This constant practice at such a young age must have helped perfect his hand–eye coordination and his shots.

After his early morning practice sessions, Victor headed off to school, where he played more cricket. He played scratch games in the playground at morning tea and lunch, and played in the school team on Friday afternoons. At Crown Street Superior School he met future Test captain Monty Noble. In his book *The Game's The Thing*, Noble wrote, 'My first recollection of Trumper was at school. He came just as I was leaving. A short, spare, narrow shouldered boy, he did not inspire one with the idea of athleticism in any direction, yet it was not long before some of the old brigade were asking: Have you seen Trumper

playing for Crown Street School? He is going to be a champion.'
By the time Trumper finished school he was already playing for
New South Wales.

Like most cricketers who go on to play for Australia, Trumper
started playing in men's competitions while still in his early teens.
This accelerated his development by challenging him to improve
his skills and concentration against tougher, more experienced
opponents. This suited Trumper, who had a will to succeed that
matched his natural gifts. Besides playing inter-school matches,
Victor never played junior cricket. At the age of 14, he turned
out for the Carlton club's second XI where he came under the
guidance of ex-internationals Charles and Alec Bannerman.

Trumper was lucky with his mentors: the Bannermans at
Carlton; Syd Gregory at South Sydney; and Monty Noble at
Paddington. The Bannermans were the first of this illustrious
group to spot Trumper's talent. Charles Bannerman scored Test
cricket's first ton – 165 retired hurt in the Melbourne Test of 1877.
Alec, a less flamboyant player, acquired the nickname 'Barndoor',
for his stonewalling abilities. The Bannerman brothers found
it hard to control the free-spirited nature of the boy Trumper.
S. H. Bowden, writing in *Town and Country Journal* in January
1913, recalled Charles Bannerman urging Trumper in the nets
to 'Leave it alone, Vic; that wasn't a ball to go at.' After a while
they realised Trumper was unique, and that 'Leave it alone' was
a comment best applied more generally to Vic's talent.

Part of Trumper's appeal was his naturalness. English captain
C.B. Fry said of him: 'He has no style, and yet is all style. He has
no fixed canonical method of play, he defies all the orthodox
rules, yet every stroke he plays satisfies the ultimate criterion
of style – minimum of effort, maximum of effect.' Trumper
believed that attack was the best form of defence. One of his

maxims was 'Spoil a bowler's length and you've got him.' Vic was disciplined in his training, but not in his shot selection. He would often try to hit the first ball for four, or hit extravagant shots off balls others would treat with caution. Like a lot of Australia's great cricketers, he was largely self-taught and didn't rely much on coaches. Monty Noble, who was instrumental in getting Trumper picked on his first tour to England in 1899, said, 'Victor was a law unto himself. You could talk to him and coach him; he would listen carefully, respect your advice and opinions, and, leaving you, would forget all you had told him, play as he wanted to play.'

A letter he wrote to a schoolboy in 1913 who was seeking advice about how to play the game sums up Trumper's attitude to cricket. Besides warning the young boy off tobacco and alcohol, he tells him to watch the ball carefully and to '… do it your own way for that will be the natural way for you'. Towards the end of the letter Vic adds, 'Don't let sport worry you, if it does give it up.' But while Trumper treated cricket as a game to be enjoyed, he wasn't flippant about his batting. Many of his best knocks came when his team was in trouble on difficult wickets.

In the early days of Test cricket, pitches were left uncovered, and teams would get caught on sticky or wet wickets. Johnnie Moyes, a cricket writer and broadcaster who saw both Trumper and Bradman play, said no one could equal Vic's skill on a sticky. In 1904, he played one of his finest innings on a wet wicket in a Test against England. He scored 74 out of Australia's total of 122. On the 1902 tour of England he peeled off 11 centuries in a summer considered one of the wettest on record. Jack Fingleton wrote in *The Immortal Victor Trumper* that his background helped him play well on tough wickets. 'The boys would play cricket or football in the open fields, in lanes or in back-yards.

From this type of cricket they developed an alert eye to jab down on 'shooters' or 'grubbers' and learned to get out of the way against kicking balls; it was this experience which undoubtedly led to Trumper being proficient on "stickies".'

But those early days, training regularly with his father at Moore Park, also taught him the importance of practice. Jack Fingleton said the Sydney Cricket Ground curator would especially prepare a sticky wicket for Vic to help him get used to the ball rising off a full length. 'On the edge of the strip of Sydney practice pitches Jennings used the hose freely, and before Victor went in on the good pitch he went in on the "sticky" which, under the influence of a hot sun, kicked and bucked. That was one reason Trumper was so proficient on them. He knew what to expect.'

Just as his father encouraged him to develop his skills at a young age, Vic encouraged others. Chappie Dwyer, who later became an Australian selector, recalled Trumper playing in the street with kids in Paddington after he'd made a big score at the SCG. He'd even let the young street urchins get him out to give them a bit of encouragement. When he moved to Chatswood in 1908, he built a pitch in the yard and encouraged developing players to train with him. A young Charlie Macartney lived nearby and would practise with Vic in the early mornings and late afternoons, a ritual Macartney continued at Chatswood Oval with other young Gordon cricketers after Vic died.

So what of Surry Hills today? Street cricket, like the old soap works and tanneries, has disappeared. There are too many cars on the streets now and too much al fresco dining going on outside the rows of cafes. It wouldn't be the done thing to slog a dirty tennis ball into someone's Caesar salad. The backyards are no smaller than they were when Vic grew up, so a child could still rehearse their shots. Though maybe not in the backyards of the old Trumper residences. The house at 119 Cooper Street has been knocked down; 10 Nichols Street is now a car park under a block of flats. Number 487 Crown Street is the site of a health food store, something the clean living Vic could probably tolerate. Moore Park, where Vic practised so diligently with his father every morning, is still a haven for cricket. There are countless astroturf wickets, and competition games are played non-stop in winter and summer across its wide expanse. Though these days you're more likely to see someone power walking or performing Tai Chi there at six in the morning, than belting cricket balls to their old man.

At Crown Street Public School, as Trumper's old school is known today, they still play cricket. Now just an infants and primary school, they field two teams, juniors and seniors, in the local primary school competition. On the warm April day I turned up to the school, there was no cricket being played, just a boisterous game of soccer on the asphalt. The Victor Trumper Cup, once awarded to the best cricketer in the school, no longer exists. The school has many notable old boys, including Snowy Baker, Sir Garfield Barwick, Monty Noble and Sir Nicholas Shehadie, but only Trumper's framed photograph sits on the wall of the school office. For years, every naughty child who visited the principal's office at Crown Street must have trudged past that photo of Vic, hoping the principal wouldn't belt them with the power of one of his lofted drives.

Charlie Macartney

PITCH: Dirt, coir matting, asphalt, wooden and turf pitches.

BAT: Home-made bats, borrowed bats and packing-case timber bats.

BALL: Apples, potatoes and hard compo balls.

WICKET: Tins, and bags of chaff.

PLAYERS: Charlie, brother Harold, schoolmates, workmates, Victor Trumper and Towser the dog.

HAZARDS: Hard balls, no gloves and pads.

PLAYERS' COMFORT LEVEL: Tough, uncompromising conditions that produced a tough, uncompromising cricketer.

Charlie Macartney's first memory of cricket was as a five-year-old, facing up to his grandfather on the family orchard near Maitland. George Moore, who played first-class cricket for New South Wales against the likes of W.G. Grace, bowled green apples at his grandson. It's not recorded how many apples young Charlie smashed to bits with his home-made cedar bat, but we do know he went on to become one of the most destructive batsmen Australia ever produced, treating most deliveries as if they were pieces of fruit.

Charlie Macartney still holds the record for the fastest triple century in first-class cricket in terms of balls faced. Playing for Australia against Notts in 1921, he plundered 345 in less than four hours. His 300 came off just 221 balls. After bringing up his 200 in 143 minutes, he called for his heavy bat, saying it was time to 'have a dip' at the bowlers. R.C. Robertson-Glasgow wrote, 'No Australian batsman, not even Bradman, has approached him for insolence of attack. He made slaves of bowlers.'

Along with Trumper, Bradman and Majid Khan, Macartney is one of only four batsmen to score a century before lunch on the first day of a Test match. But Macartney's effort stands alone in that he achieved it at the age of 40 on a wet wicket, knocking up 112 not out before the break. At the age of 45, he was still giving bowlers hell. In a first-grade match against Paddington in 1931/2 he clubbed 94 runs in just 32 minutes.

Charlie Macartney may have been cavalier on the field, but he was more Calvinist off it. A churchgoer and non-drinker, he preached the benefits of hard work. 'All through my boyhood days cricket practice was supreme,' he wrote in *My Cricketing Days*. 'No time nor opportunity was allowed to pass without practice in one way or another, and even at that early age, my great ambition was to be one of an Australian Eleven.'

Peter Sharpham, author of *Charlie Macartney: Cricket's Governor-General*, argues this hunger for practice was forged from disappointment. At the age of around nine or ten, Macartney was competing with another schoolboy to make it into the local village eleven. He missed out and watched the game from underneath a pepper tree, despondent at his non-selection.

Sharpham believes this was a formative moment in Macartney's cricket career. 'Such dismay helps mould the boy into manhood and strengthens the resolve of future champions,' Sharpham writes. 'For weeks after the match he practised batting, bowling and fielding during every spare minute to ensure he was included in future sides.'

In May 1898, the Macartneys left the Maitland district and moved to Sydney. Charlie was soon playing pick-up games on dirt wickets at Queens Park, a few kilometres from the Sydney Cricket Ground. The boys there used a bat and a hard ball, but had little else in the way of equipment. 'Our only protection was the skin which covered our knuckles and bones,' Macartney recalled. Each Christmas young Charlie was given a home-made bat by his father. But these bats were better suited to hitting apples than cricket balls. Without a cane handle to reinforce it, they snapped under the strain of Charlie's sizzling strokeplay. Luckily one of the other Queens Park boys was given a five-shilling bat by his mother. It was a good investment; the bat was shared amongst the boys, and ensured they could keep playing competitive games with a hard ball.

Charlie would do anything to get a game of cricket. At one stage he was caught out taking two weeks off from classes at Woollahra Superior Public School to work on his cricket. When his father found out, he packed him off to Fort Street Model School. To the dismay of young Macartney, Fort Street didn't field a cricket team that year. The headmaster Mr J.W. Turner had cancelled cricket for the season after poor results in the yearly examinations. Charlie soon got over this trauma. In 1900, the family relocated to Chatswood, then a bush suburb on the North Shore of Sydney. It proved a good move for Charlie's cricket. Chatswood Public School had a team, Chatswood Oval had just been built, and a batting genius later moved into the neighbourhood and Charlie's orbit.

Chatswood Oval has been the home of Gordon's first-grade team since 1905. Since then some of the most watchable batsmen in Australian cricket history have played for the Stags, including Victor Trumper, Johnny Taylor, Sid Barnes, Neil Harvey and Adam Gilchrist. When the Macartneys moved in up the road, the Gordon club didn't exist. A turf pitch had been laid and was tended to painstakingly by players and officials from the Willoughby District Cricket Club. When they realised two young boys were getting on their newly laid pitch for early morning practice sessions, they alerted the local constabulary. As a consequence, Charlie and his elder brother Harold had to get up very early to practise on that centre wicket.

Morning practice sessions became a ritual for Charlie Macartney. Jack Fingleton wrote in *Masters of Cricket*: 'In summer he never varied his habit – not even when he was playing in a Test – of arriving at Chatswood Oval (in Sydney) at 6.40 and leaving at 7.50 on five days a week. Some 17 Gordon members went to this early morning practice and Macartney found that the pace of a composition ball skidding off a dewy pitch was ideal for sharpening up his eyesight and his strokes.' In the early days, Charlie and Harold took their dog Towser with them to chase the ball. As Charlie put it, Towser 'enabled us to hit as hard and often as we chose'. It was good practice for Charlie's future strokeplay at Chatswood Oval, where he later caused havoc on the nearby bowling green with his big hitting.

Charlie's daily practice sessions started to pay off. He scored an undefeated 121 out of 219 in a school game and then cleaned up the opposition with 7/1. He impressed Monty Noble, the legendary Australian all-rounder, when he turned up at school to do some coaching. Noble retold the story in the *Sydney Mail* in 1921. 'One little chap who came briskly to the wicket was so diminutive that I eased up my pace to give him a show. He stood up to my bowling with such confidence and played it so easily that I quickened up. Still he went on, cutting, driving and pulling so readily that I soon had my vest off. I pegged away for all I was worth, but the little fellow finished his batting time undefeated.' It wasn't just Macartney's batting that impressed. Given an opportunity to bowl a few of his left-arm spinners at Noble, he soon knocked his stumps over.

In 1902, Charlie left school and got a job as a junior clerk in a produce store near the wharves on Sussex Street. He kept practising his cricket, even in his lunch hour. In keeping with a long tradition of workplace productivity on the docks, every lunch-time one of the local wharves was turned temporarily into a cricket pitch. A proper bat and ball were used, and a hessian bag filled with chaff was the wicket. The wharf was made of hardwood planks that were laid unevenly. The hard ball deviated sharply off the gaps between the planks, testing the reflexes and shinbones of anyone game enough to bat. No doubt there were plenty of wharfies queuing up to dig a few into the ribs of the young clerk Macartney.

During work hours, Charlie had to do some heavy lifting himself, loading wool bales for his employer. This manual labour on the docks helped develop his strength, something that was crucial to his batting. As Sharpham wrote, '. . . he had exceptionally strong wrists and a broad chest. Combined with an unusually long reach and exceptionally fast footwork, either in the field or the batting crease, Macartney proved to be an intimidating and forceful opponent.'

In the same year Macartney left school, he started playing

grade for North Sydney. By the time he was picked in the third-grade team aged 16 he'd been playing in men's competitions since the age of 12. Like his later mentor Victor Trumper, Macartney played no junior cricket besides school cricket. He described his cricket apprenticeship as a 'hard school'. Captains were tough on young players and you were picked according to your performances. North Sydney was a very strong club. All of their first-grade team at one stage played for New South Wales. When Charlie made it into second-grade as a 17-year-old, he shared the spinning duties with H.V. 'Ranji' Horden. Both would go on to win Test matches for Australia with their bowling, yet they couldn't crack the firsts. In early 1905, Macartney finally got a game in first-grade, but only when opening batsmen Reggie Duff and Bert Hopkins went to England with the Australian side.

In 1905/1906, the Gordon District Cricket Club was formed. Charlie Macartney went straight into their first-grade side and could bat on that centre wicket at Chatswood Oval all he liked. A few years later, Victor Trumper moved to Chatswood and played for Gordon. Like Macartney, Trumper believed in hard work and had been doing early morning practice sessions since he was a boy. Trumper had a turf pitch installed at his father's home in Help Street and Charlie was invited around to practise.

Macartney acknowledged the huge influence Trumper had on the way he played the game. 'For numerous hints and batting examples, I owe more than I can say to Victor Trumper.' Macartney's stance was like Trumper's, and he learned how to play some of his mentor's more unorthodox strokes like the yorker shot where he lifted a leg and hit a yorker to the square-leg boundary. One of Trumper's favourite sayings was 'Spoil a bowler's length and you've got him'. Arthur Mailey, who suffered at the hands of both batsmen, recognised the same attitude in

Macartney. 'Brimful of confidence, he would boast of his capacity to knock a bowler right off his length.'

As part of Trumper's plan to knock a bowler off his length, he would try and hit the first ball in a new spell for four. Macartney took this to new levels. Jack Fingleton once opened the batting with Macartney and was told, 'Keep your eyes open for the first ball'. Fingleton thought this meant get ready for a quick single. Instead Macartney blasted back a straight drive that sent the bowler, the umpire and Fingleton ducking for cover. 'We were all prone on the ground, as if in an air-raid, as the ball crashed into the pickets.' After Fingleton had dusted himself off and met Macartney halfway down the pitch, he was told 'It's always a good idea to aim the first ball right here at the bowler's head. They don't like it. It rattles 'em.'

Macartney did rattle the bowlers, but mostly in the second part of his career. He originally justified his place in the Test team as a bowling all-rounder, taking 11/85 against England in Leeds in 1909. In his first 22 Tests he scored just one century. Macartney lost many of his best years to World War I. He served with the AIF in France and didn't play a Test match between 1912 and 1920. After the war he became increasingly adventurous, batting more and more like Trumper. Before the war he averaged 26.63 with the bat from 21 Tests. Post war he averaged 69.55 from 14 Tests. After his 100 before lunch at Headingley in 1926, Sir Pelham Warner felt Macartney had in that innings eclipsed his mentor, 'I say without hesitation that I have never seen a greater innings. Not even the immortal Trumper could have played more finely.' Macartney's swashbuckling 170 in the Sydney Test of 1921 inspired a young Don Bradman who was attending his first Test match.

Macartney was an original. His background of dirt wickets, orchards and wooden wharves helped him adapt to batting in any situation. He had good mentors. His grandfather gave him his first taste for the game and, in Trumper, he had the best possible teacher. He had the dedication to match his skill level. He practised so often that batting was something he could do in his sleep. These days even professional cricketers would struggle to train as regularly as Macartney did. It certainly doesn't happen anymore at Chatswood Oval. Graham King, a historian and former player with the Gordon club, thinks this habit was kicked by at least the 1940s. He recalls his captain calling for a one-off morning training session during a semi-final series back in the 1970s. Two players turned up, he and the captain. Macartney repeated his training ritual every morning for years. No wonder he was so good.

Arthur Mailey

PITCH: Streets and local parks.

BAT: Whatever they could find in the neighbourhood.

BALL: Oranges, tennis balls, cricket balls.

PLAYERS: Would play by himself and with neighbourhood kids.

HAZARDS: Mean streets full of larrikin gangs.

BACKYARD DRILLS: Bowling the orange in the dining room at home.

PLAYERS' COMFORT LEVEL: Unimaginable conditions. Born and raised in a slum full of disease and violence.

Arthur Mailey did well to survive his upbringing, let alone play cricket for Australia. Born in 1886 in Waterloo, one of the worst of Sydney's slums, he was one of eight children. At the time, infant mortality rates in Sydney were worse than London, with suburbs like Waterloo leading the misery. Sydney's population nearly trebled between 1870 and 1890 and amenities hadn't kept up. Waterloo, built around sand hills and a swamp, was prone to sandstorms and flies, mosquitoes and disease. Houses were overcrowded and sanitation was poor. Two of the Mailey children didn't make it past two. And for those who did make it, the prospects were frequently grim. Waterloo was known for its gangs of unemployed youths. Just months before Arthur was born, members of the Waterloo Push gang-raped a 16-year-old orphan named Mary Jane Hicks in the sand hills of nearby Mount Rennie. Four of them were hanged for their crime.

A lack of building regulations meant any old house could be knocked up in no time at all. The Mailey house, *Alma Cottage*, was built on the slope of a sand hill. It was a wooden house with hessian-lined walls. As more Mailey children were born, more rooms were tacked on out the back. On the walls of Arthur's bedroom was a picture of his hero Victor Trumper. 'During the winter the hessian partitions bellied and flapped like the sails of a ship in distress and clouds of sand blew through the cracks of the floor,' Mailey recalled in his memoir *10 for 66 and All That*. 'When the wind blew, Vic appeared to go through his whole repertoire of strokes.'

Mailey's father, John, spent much of the family income at the pub. The demon drink didn't just have an influence on Mailey's home life, it affected his cricket as well. 'I lived in the same world as the boy next door or the beer-sodden hag down the lane who screeched, "Willie! come 'ome, you young b------, and get my beer before the pub shuts." The terrified Willie would drop the home-made bat and race home like a hare. I hated the woman not because of her thirst but because she had deprived me of somebody to practise my bowling on.'

It seems young Arthur couldn't have bowled to his father either, even if he was sober. 'My father didn't know the first thing about cricket ... As far as I know nobody on either side of my family had played *any* game, let alone cricket.' Given the environment and family Mailey grew up in, even he seemed surprised he made it as a cricketer. 'My environment, from the days when instinct and reason were suspicious of each other, pointed the way to crime or at least the life of a confidence man, rather than that of a cricketer.'

But smack bang in the middle of Waterloo, Mailey was to learn the trick that would make him cricket's version of the confidence man – the bosie bowler. The bosie, also known as the googly, or the wrong 'un, was brought to Australia by its inventor, B. J. Bosanquet, in 1903. Bowled with a leg-spin action, it turns the other way, perplexing batsmen. Photos of Mailey bowling in his prime show him concealing his grip behind his back till the very last moment, hiding his tricks from his victims, like one of those scam artists from the streets of Waterloo.

Like most boys in his neighbourhood, Mailey had little formal education. He left Waterloo Public School at 13 and got a job pressing trousers. There he encountered a boss he described as 'the meanest man I ever knew'. He was soon sacked for leaning against the pressing board, daydreaming. What was he thinking about? 'Victor Trumper as usual, I fancy.' Out of work, Mailey had time on his hands. He would walk three miles to the Domain, where men who worked in the nearby offices would have a hit in the nets. 'Anything to be near cricket,' as he put it. He was also close to his other great love, art. He would head over to the Art Gallery of NSW and look at his favourite paintings 'Rorke's Drift', 'The Scoffers' and 'Visit of the Queen of Sheba to King Solomon'. Mailey later developed his artistic skills drawing cartoons and caricatures for Australian and English newspapers.

In one of those out-of-work journeys to and from the Domain, Mailey had his Eureka moment. As he was walking past Waterloo Park, depressed at his lot in life, Mailey saw a group of boys playing cricket. One of them was bowling bosies. At first

Mailey was baffled by the delivery and couldn't work out how it was bowled, but he joined in the game and learned through observation. 'I cottoned onto it after a time and rushed home like somebody who had found a nugget of gold.' It's unknown who the young boy was who taught Mailey to bowl bosies, but maybe they ought to erect a statue in his honour. This game of park cricket led to a chain of events in Australian cricket that helped them dominate England in Ashes series for generations to come. Mailey took 36 wickets against England in 1920/1921. Mailey inspired Clarrie Grimmett as well as inadvertently teaching Bill O'Reilly how to bowl wrong 'uns. O'Reilly had a big influence on Richie Benaud's bowling. Benaud passed his knowledge down the line to a series of leg-spinners, including Shane Warne.

Mailey practised his new weapon day and night, sometimes in the dining room at home. 'What little crockery we possessed was smashed to pieces.' He didn't have a ball so he used oranges. He was playing junior cricket at the time in a local paddock, but he didn't have the nerve to unleash the bosie in a game. At the same time, Mailey's lack of employment was getting him down. Unskilled and uneducated, he struggled to pick up anything much more than casual labouring jobs. At one point in his teenage years he even gave up cricket and spent a summer fishing with his mother and his crippled brother. The man who stills holds the best ever bowling figures by an Australian in a Test innings, could easily have quit the game at this early stage.

Quality leg-spin bowling is beautiful to watch, but it can be brutal to bowl. It's not a trade best pursued by men with soft hands or soft underbellies. It takes a lot of practice to perfect leg-spinners and their variations. One of the original bosie bowlers, Aubrey Faulkner, said it took him five years to master the leg-break and the googly. Clarrie Grimmett worked on his flipper, day and night, summer and winter for 12 years before he dared bowl it in a match. Bowling leg-spinners for long spells rips the skin off your spinning fingers. For bowlers like Mailey, who try to bowl big leg-breaks, it can be a career-threatening problem. Colin McCool was ruled out of an Ashes Test on the 1948 tour after Don Bradman spied his red raw fingers at breakfast on the morning of a match.

Mailey's background helped him overcome this problem before it even began. At the age of 16, he started a job as a glassblower that had a lasting effect on his bowling. 'The continual spinning of the four-foot pipe which held the molten glass gave me fingers of great strength and toughness,' Mailey recalled in *10 for 66 and All That*. Jack Fingleton said that Mailey could break the ball more than any man he knew and Mailey thought this had a lot to do with his time spent at the bottle works. 'When bowling, my fingers never became calloused, worn or tired, and this I feel, was responsible for the fact that I never met a bowler who could spin the ball more viciously than I …' Mailey was true to his word. Even if bowlers got after him, he could bowl long spells. When Victoria racked up a world record 1107 in a Sheffield Shield match in 1926, he bowled 64 eight-ball overs.

At the bottle works, Mailey practised against the wall during smokos and lunch breaks. A strike eventually shut down the bottle works and put Mailey out of work again. But by then he was back in the swing of cricket. He got a job painting a house near Botany Bay and was paid not in money but in willow – a cricket bat that once belonged to Victor Trumper. 'This was another link closer to the great batsman and I was more than ever determined to improve my bowling.' Mailey was obsessed by Trumper. He hung outside the SCG in the hope of getting a glimpse of him. Once he hopped on a tram without a ticket so he could sit opposite his hero. He did so only for three stops, fearing a boot up the bum from the conductor. Mailey eventually made his way up the grades at Redfern and eventually got Trumper out in a first-grade match. As he famously described the event, 'There was no triumph in me as I watched the receding figure. I felt like a boy who had killed a dove.'

Arthur Mailey went on to take 99 wickets for Australia from 21 Tests. Australia only lost two of the games he played in. His figures of 9/121 are still the best by an Australian in a Test match innings. These days Waterloo remains a tough area, but nothing like the environment in which Mailey grew up. Having a hit in Portman Street today would be hard work, but a young leg-spinner could still practise trouble-free in the lane where Mailey's old home backs onto. Waterloo Park, where Mailey discovered his bosie, still exists. It's got a turf pitch and is the home of the Paddington District Cricket Club, Trumper's old club, which now plays in the City and Suburban competition. Mailey believed that if he could play for Australia, anyone could. As he wrote in *10 for 66 and All That*: 'Why did I write this book? Perhaps I am really hoping that it will give strength and encouragement to those who feel that nothing can be gained without outside help; that the Test arena is a sanctuary for the privileged; that one must be nursed, schooled and coached in order to play in big cricket. It is possible, I understand, to obtain a passport to Heaven; but a passport to cricket is not to be had, and even if one were forged, the romance, the struggle, the adventure and the friendship would be missing.'

Clarrie Grimmett

PITCH: Home-made turf pitch.

BAT: Not required, but if someone wanted to face up he had an old Jack Hobbs bat handy.

BALL: Eight worn cricket balls, plus tennis balls and ping-pong balls for experimentation.

WICKET: One wooden stump.

PLAYERS: Clarrie and Joe the fox terrier.

PLAYERS' COMFORT LEVEL: No discomfort, more of a Zen-like state of bliss. Bowled in backyard till the age of 76.

For Clarrie Grimmett, backyard cricket wasn't a carefree game played in the endless summers of one's youth. For starters he grew up in New Zealand, where endless cloud-cover is more the stuff of childhood memories. As a boy, he played mainly in the street or at the local park. Clarrie Grimmett's backyard cricket was played as an adult. At the age of 28, struggling to make it into first-class cricket, he laid a turf pitch in his backyard. It was here that he relentlessly set about perfecting the art of leg-spin bowling, experimenting with new deliveries and perfecting old ones. It's hard to imagine a cricketer who bowled more balls in the backyard than Clarrie. He was still at it in his late seventies.

Clarrie Grimmett was born on 25 December 1891. His bowling comrade Bill O'Reilly later described him as the best Christmas present Australia ever received from New Zealand. As a six-year-old living in Wellington, he would head down to nearby Basin Reserve and play cricket with the Harris brothers, three older boys who lived next door in Roxburgh Street. The Harris boys bowled leg-spin and passed their passion on to young Clarrie. Basin Reserve must've been a little rougher back then. With their kit, the boys packed a spade so they could smooth out any bumps in their outfield pitch. If Clarrie and the Harris boys wanted a truer surface there was always their street that provided plenty of bounce and turn for aspiring leg-spinners. The only obstacles on this asphalt pitch were the odd horse and cart and the local policeman. As Ashley Mallett recounted in *Clarrie Grimmett, The Bradman of Spin* once Constable Thirsk arrived, 'These cricket-mad urchins of Wellington would scatter in all directions.'

Young Clarrie loved to spin the ball. He got a thrill from watching the ball dip in the air and fizz off the pitch. But he worried he would be belted out of the attack if he bowled leg-spin in a real match. As a schoolboy at Mount Cook Boys High he bowled fast. One day towards the end of a school practice session, he sent down a few of his leg-spinners. His sportsmaster Mr Hempelmann was so impressed he told him he was never to bowl fast again. But next game Clarrie ignored his advice. Mr Hempelmann had left early to meet his brother at the docks and Clarrie decided to come in off the long run. He took 7/3, and hit one player in the head. After this demolition job he was picked for Wellington Schools to play Wairarapa Schools. Mr Hempelmann heard that Clarrie had disobeyed him. The sportsmaster was not impressed. He made it clear to Clarrie that he must bowl his leggies.

Playing for Wellington Schools, Grimmett was stuck in a quandary. Did he obey his sportsmaster? Or bowl the kind of deliveries he'd been selected for in the first place? He probably worked out that he'd have to deal with Hempelmann more often than the Wellington Schools selectors. Taking the new ball, he shocked his captain and the rest of his team mates by bowling a leg-break first up. The batsman played and missed. Grimmett stuck at his leg-spinners. He took 6/5 in the first innings and 8/1 in the second. Clarrie's son Vic still has the score sheet at his home in Adelaide. Australian cricket owes much to 'Dimp' Hempelmann's intervention.

Once he was out of the leg-spinning closet, Clarrie was able to work full time on his craft. He soon realised bowling just leg-breaks was not enough, and added a top-spinner and a bosie to his repertoire. His progress stalled temporarily when, like Mailey and Bradman, he took time off from competition cricket in his teens, but some sensible friends soon dragged him down to the nets and got him bowling again. By the age of 20, he'd made his first-class debut – quite young for a leg-spinner. But in those days New Zealand were a long way off achieving Test cricket status. If Grimmett was to further his career he had to leave home. In May 1914, aged 22, he sailed to Australia.

Clarrie Grimmett played grade cricket in Sydney for three seasons, but with Arthur Mailey playing for New South Wales, opportunities were scarce. In 1917, Clarrie moved to Victoria and played for South Melbourne. After marrying Elizabeth Egan in 1919, he bought a house at Caulfield and joined Prahran. The move was good for Clarrie's cricket. The house at 30 Lockhart Street, Caulfield had a big backyard. He built a full-sized cricket pitch with enough room for a short run up. Jack Fingleton wrote that he specially ordered Merri Creek soil, the same soil the MCG pitch was made of at the time.

Clarrie was obsessive about his backyard training sessions. Each day, no matter the weather conditions, he found two hours, either before or after work, to practise his bowling. In the Grimmett household there was no such thing as the cricket season. Clarrie practised all year round. While team mates were playing football or taking a break, Clarrie was trying to get ahead, working on his stock ball and experimenting with new deliveries. All this was done within the privacy of his backyard, away from the prying eyes of batsmen. He did have one colleague he regularly practised with. His name was Joe and he was a black-and-white fox terrier. Joe was trained to fetch the balls, increasing the efficiency of Grimmett's daily sessions.

Joe became one of Grimmett's best allies in cricket. Clarrie taught him to lie down next to the wicket for the duration of an over. Joe then jumped up, picked up all the balls and returned them to the bowler's end in time for Clarrie to send down another over. On Sundays, Clarrie allowed some local cricketers to come over and use his pitch. One day, a young Bill Ponsford, then just a district cricketer in Melbourne, saw Joe's trick and said, 'That dog might be famous one day, yer know.' Joe the fox terrier certainly proved smarter than the Victorian selection committee. Grimmett took 228 wickets at 12.93 in the four seasons he played for Prahran. In that time he played just two games for Victoria.

Desperate to play regular first-class cricket, Clarrie took up an offer from South Australia and moved his family to Adelaide in May 1924. He soon proved a success at first-class level. The following year he was picked to play his first Test, at the age of 33. Given how long it took him to make it, you'd understand if Grimmett was overcome by the occasion. But not so. 'I was thrilled at being given the ball but I was not really nervous because I have always had supreme confidence in my bowling and in my ability to maintain a length.' Grimmett took 11/82 in his Test debut. His victims included Jack Hobbs, Frank Woolley and Patsy Hendren, the three highest ever run scorers in first-class cricket. All that practice in the backyard with Joe was paying off. Unlike other leg-spinners, who struggled with accuracy, Grimmett could land the ball on the spot from the get-go.

Bowling a cricket ball can be a painfully complex exercise. You need to grip the ball in the correct fashion and get your run up right. Your feet need to land in the right place, and your arms must follow. Your point of delivery has to be mechanically sound as you release the ball. If your head, your arms, or your legs are even slightly in the wrong place, your bowling radar goes askew. There are so many points at which a bowler's action can fall down. But when it all clicks it's a thing of beauty, known in the bowling fraternity as rhythm. When you've got your rhythm, you're in an almost meditative state where bowling seems the most natural thing in the world.

But attaining that elusive rhythm takes a lot of hard work. Bowling is one of the most unnatural things you can do in sport. It's not like running or kicking or catching or throwing. Nothing else in day-to-day life prepares you for it. The challenge for bowlers is to make what seems so unnatural, seem natural. Bill O'Reilly used to say you need to reach the state where you can run up and deliver a ball blindfolded. Clarrie Grimmett practised so hard and so often on his backyard pitches it became instinctual. Whenever he bowled, wherever he bowled, he could land the ball exactly where he wanted to.

Not that Clarrie's daily training sessions were turning him into a line-and-length robot. Clarrie's backyard pitch was as much a backyard laboratory as it was a drill ground for leg-spin. He experimented with various deliveries using cricket balls, tennis balls and ping-pong balls. It was within this environment that he invented one of cricket's most potent deliveries – the flipper, a ball that Richie Benaud and Shane Warne also came to master.

Grimmett worked on the flipper in the backyard for more than a decade. 'For twelve years I practised this ball before I bowled it in a match. Let that be an example to a youngster! It proved to be my greatest ball. I called it my "flipper". I had to perfect it before allowing the batsman to sample it.' Some batsmen said they could pick Grimmett's flipper because it came accompanied with a flicking sound. But the old fox always stayed a step ahead. When he heard this piece of information was being shared among batsmen, he started clicking the fingers on his left hand while bowling his leg-breaks.

Grimmett took 216 wickets in 37 Tests, close to six wickets per Test. That's on average, one wicket a Test match better than Shane Warne. Grimmett would've taken many more wickets if selectors hadn't been so slow to recognise his ability and so fast to curtail his career. In Grimmett's last series in 1935/6 he took 44 wickets in just five Tests. Selectors omitted him from the 1938 tour to England much to the disgust of his old bowling chum Bill O'Reilly. In the 1939/40 domestic season, at the age of 47, he took a record 73 wickets in nine games. After that season, the war intervened and Clarrie's career was officially over, but he kept experimenting in the backyard. Jack Fingleton told the story in *Fingleton on Cricket* of a chance encounter during the war between Grimmett and the great cricket writer Neville Cardus.

'This is a terrible thing, this war, Neville,' said Clarrie.

'It is, indeed,' readily agreed Neville, 'when we think of all the art and culture it has left in ruins throughout Europe. The lovely old historic buildings, the –'

'Yes, yes,' hastily cut in Grimmett, 'I know all about that. I was thinking particularly of a new ball I had discovered. I'll never have the chance now to try it out against class batsmen.'

Grimmett never did get to try out that new delivery in first-class cricket. By the time the war was over and the Sheffield Shield resumed he was 54. But he never lost the hunger for trying new things. Right up until his late seventies he was bowling on his backyard pitch at 109 Glynde Road, Firle, training young players and experimenting with new deliveries. According to Ashley Mallett, who trained on Grimmett's backyard pitch, Clarrie was working on a ball he called the wrong wrong 'un at the age of 76: '… the wrist was turned so far round that the ball actually came from the crooked wrist as a leg-break. Clarrie could bowl it, but only over a distance of roughly 10 metres.'

The two backyard pitches where Clarrie spent so much time perfecting his craft no longer exist. The house at Firle was demolished to make way for a supermarket. A plaque in the car park marks the place where Clarrie used to practise his craft. In Caulfield, the big block where Clarrie first cultivated a pitch has been subdivided. A second house now takes up the space where Grimmett, Ponsford and Joe the fox terrier used to practise.

But if Clarrie was around today, the rise of battleaxe blocks and supermarket developments wouldn't have stopped him. He would've gone bush if he had to. Clarrie would have found a way to train his two hours a day, and perfect the art form that saw him become one of the greatest ever leg-spin bowlers.

Dogs

Clarrie Grimmett's dog, Joe, was a leg-spinner's best friend. Clarrie was able to bowl more deliveries each time he practised, thanks to Joe's fetching ability. But sadly the little black-and-white fox terrier met his maker prematurely. Some time after the Grimmett family moved from Melbourne to Adelaide, Joe disappeared. 'Apparently he was poisoned,' Grimmett wrote. 'At any rate, I never saw my friend again, although my son and I spent many hours tramping the streets in search of him.'

• • •

Joe wasn't the only dog to help maximise the efficiency of a prospective Test cricketer's training methods. Charlie Macartney used to take his dog Towser down to Chatswood Oval for his morning practice sessions. Towser allowed Charlie and his brother Harold to practise a full range of strokes. 'We had a very fine dog,' Macartney wrote, 'which was quite as good as a fielding side, and when we were alone, as was mostly the case, the work of Towser enabled us to hit as hard and often as we chose.'

• • •

The Chappell family's dog was more in the line of fire than Joe or Towser. Champ was an enthusiastic participant in Ian, Greg and Trevor's backyard battles, and was taught to field the ball and drop it back at the bowler's feet. The cross beagle/ kelpie was as safe a catcher as any of the Chappell boys, particularly in the arc between cover and mid-on. But playing against the brothers with a hard ball could prove a dangerous assignment. One day, Greg thumped an on-drive in the air within Champ's orbit. The dog took a screamer, but was groggy for a while afterwards. The catch had loosened a couple of Champ's teeth.

Family dogs have greatly assisted upcoming fast bowlers. Perhaps they have an innate empathy for the downtrodden and done over. Dennis Lillee's neighbour's dog acted as boundary rider in their local games. Ray Lindwall's street games in Hurstville were made easier thanks to an alsatian who kept wickets. Keith Miller's dog, Buttons, was considered the best fielder in the family backyard games at Elsternwick.

• • •

Geoff Lawson's black labrador Skipper retrieved shots where no other fielder was brave enough to go. 'Next door was full of bindi-eyes,' Lawson recalls, 'and the dog, well, he was a bit reluctant to pick up a ball full of bindi-eyes, but he used to do a pretty good job.' Skipper's water bowl, a cut-off oil drum, was also used to wet the ball. 'It was right next to the run-up,' says Lawson, 'so you could bowl with a wet skiddy ball and when you hit people it was really good. It gave a bit of a sting.' A dog that helps facilitate the inflicting of pain on a batsman? That truly is a fast bowler's best friend.

Bill O'Reilly

PITCH: Tennis court, back paddock, or out the front of the house.

BAT: Normal cricket bat.

BALL: Tennis ball or a chiselled down banksia root.

WICKET: Gatepost out the front.

PLAYERS: Bill and his six siblings.

BACKYARD DRILLS: Bowling at the gatepost.

PLAYERS' COMFORT LEVEL: Hot bush climate and unforgiving elder siblings.

Bill O'Reilly was born to bowl long spells under the Australian sun. He arrived, the fourth child of an eventual seven, on a stinking hot December day at White Cliffs, a New South Wales mining town out the back of Bourke. Young Bill had to acclimatise fast. It was so hot his father, Ernest O'Reilly, placed wet hessian bags over the corrugated iron roof to try and make it a bit more bearable for his wife Mina and their newborn son. This was probably the first and last time conditions were made more favourable for 'Tiger' O'Reilly.

Ernest O'Reilly had lived in White Cliffs since 1896. As a trainee teacher he had to make his way each December to Hay and back for his exams, a round trip of 1000 kilometres. It's hard to believe, but he made this trip on his own, riding a primitive pushbike along dusty bush tracks in the middle of summer, relying on bore water holes to fill up his waterbag. Bill would show similar determination and hardiness, bowling to the world's best batsmen on flat decks in hot conditions. At the end of his toil, Bill at least had beer rather than bore water to quench his thirst; a substance he believed had special recuperative powers.

In 1908, the O'Reillys moved from White Cliffs to Marengo (now called Murringo). It was here that young Bill got his first real taste for cricket. The children built a tennis court between the schoolhouse and the road. The court doubled as a cricket ground. On Christmas Day 1913, Bill was given a bat. In *Tiger: 60 years of Cricket* he recalled running out onto the court still in his pyjamas and belting the first ball from his brother Jack over the wire netting fence for six. It's little wonder Bill remembered this moment fondly. It was probably one of the rare occasions he got a bat in his hand. With three older siblings, Jack, Tom and Nell, all keen cricketers, his fate was sealed – he would spend a lot of his youth bowling. As his great mate Jack Fingleton wrote, 'The dignity and the size of his elders taught the young O'Reilly to mind his place; not to give himself airs and graces; to accept a menial job, such as bowling.'

It's hard to imagine O'Reilly ever minding his place with a ball in hand, even at that young age. He became one of cricket's fiercest competitors. 'Tiger', unlike 'Dainty', 'Rowdy' and 'Slasher' was not an ironic nickname. The Tiger was a ferocious beast in combat. As R.S. Whitington wrote, 'All of O'Reilly's series were a species of private war against the batsmen.' For fellow leg-spinner, Colin McCool, O'Reilly displayed the characteristics of more than one member of the animal kingdom. 'Off the field he could be your life-long buddy, but out in the middle he had all the lovable qualities of a demented rhinoceros.'

Maybe it was in the bush at Murringo that O'Reilly developed his notorious hatred of batsmen. Bowling unsuccessfully at older siblings in hot conditions was an unforgiving exercise. Being the fourth child meant he probably didn't get many favourable umpiring decisions either. Fingleton wrote that O'Reilly spent much of his youth bowling with a 'tough, gnarled Banksia tree root. They took it in turns to work on the root with a chisel and in time it came to resemble a ball.' Conditions weren't always this prehistoric. O'Reilly eventually graduated to a tennis ball. But he learned fast that bowlers often got the rough end of the stick. A boy who empathised with his father and his marathon bike rides to Hay was unlikely to side with cricket's most pampered species – the batsmen. Popular and protected, in O'Reilly's view they always had the laws, the conditions and the administrators on their side.

From his childhood on O'Reilly wanted to steamroll batsmen. If they weren't going to do the right thing and get out, he'd torture them till they did. Denis Compton said he felt 'wrung out' after facing O'Reilly for just an hour. Don Bradman described hitting O'Reilly for four as like disturbing a hive of bees. When Len Hutton scored a then record 365 against Australia in 1938, all of the Australians congratulated him on the field except O'Reilly. 'The day I congratulate a batsman in the middle of the field you can carry me off feet first,' he said. 'I can congratulate them at the bar.' As R.C. Robertson-Glasgow said about O'Reilly, 'He looked as if, under necessary circumstances, he might have founded or sacked a city.'

The cricket beatings O'Reilly weathered at the hands of older siblings at Murringo did him a favour. They toughened him up without diminishing his desire. In 1917, the O'Reilly family moved to Wingello, a small but cricket obsessed town around 50 kilometres from Goulburn. At Wingello, Bill channelled his competitive spirit into organised cricket. His first game was against Tallong Juniors, played at Hatter's Paddock. The pre-match warm up consisted of an 11-kilometre walk to the ground. O'Reilly remembered the game more for being bitten by a 'Jumping Joey' ant while scoring, than for any great deeds on the pitch. While at Wingello, O'Reilly experienced two crucial events that helped set him on the path to becoming a Test cricketer. He met a young schoolmaster at Goulburn High, Bob Golding, who convinced him to stick to spin bowling and not bowl fast. And he received a critical letter in the mail from his big brother Jack.

Jack O'Reilly had left Wingello and moved to Sydney to take up a job at the Agriculture Department. He played cricket with North Sydney in their third-grade side. Arthur Mailey, at that stage, was Australia's star leg-spin bowler, having just taken a record 36 wickets in a series against England. Mailey was invited by the North Sydney committee to come along to one of their afternoon practice sessions. Jack placed himself strategically behind the nets and watched Mailey's action carefully. He wrote a letter to Bill detailing how he thought Mailey was bowling his bosie or wrong 'un. It was the moment that Bill later described as the most important occurrence in his cricketing life.

Bill had been enthralled by the idea of the bosie since he first read about it in the papers during Mailey's record-breaking series of 1920–21. But no one could explain to him how it was done. He could not even learn from watching the best exponents of this rare art. TV was several decades away and he didn't see a first-class game until he was 19. For Bill, Jack's letter was the key to unlocking the secrets of the mystery ball that he so desperately wanted to bowl. But Jack O'Reilly hadn't spoken to Mailey about his grip, his action, or his delivery. He was only describing what he saw. And what he saw was something even England's best batsmen had trouble reading. In a letter that led to more torment for the MCC, Jack observed that every time Mailey bowled his bosie he dropped his wrist and the ball seemed to come out of the back of the hand.

It was hardly a Bosies for Dummies step-by-step guide. But it was enough information for Bill. Within a few days of receiving the letter he taught himself to change the spin from anti-clockwise to clockwise without any discernible change to his action. Bill was around 15 at the time. He practised the delivery 'day in, day out, winter and summer alike'. His target was an old wooden gatepost. '… as soon as I got it into my repertoire I didn't let up, I bowled at our old front gate post, I'll guarantee the post got sick and tired of looking at me.' England's batsmen would soon get sick and tired of O'Reilly. His wrong 'un went on to take many Test wickets. It bounced steeply and often led to catches in close on the leg side.

This persistent bowling at the gatepost as a youth helped O'Reilly with his accuracy. For a leg-spinner he was extraordinarily consistent. He claimed he never bowled a wide in first-class cricket. Being able to bowl fast leg-spinners in an accurate yet aggressive fashion is what made O'Reilly unique. Add to that his deceptive qualities, the ability to mix up leg-spinners, top-spinners and wrong 'uns at various paces and you had an unbeatable combination.

The place where Bill O'Reilly said he learned the art of

deception might be a surprise to many. It was inside the family home, playing what O'Reilly described as 'a silly little game'. When rain came, the O'Reilly children crammed inside and played French cricket. 'That's the thing where I learned all the secrets I ever learned about hoodwinking a batsman, into getting underneath his bat, or getting caught off it because he wasn't there at the right time,' O'Reilly recalled in an interview he gave to the National Library of Australia. 'It's an enormously important lesson, it can be learned in a silly little game like French cricket, and there you get the idea of being too soon, too late, or not being there at all.' By changing his pace and varying the type of spin he put on the ball, O'Reilly was able to lead the batsmen into making mistakes.

O'Reilly claimed that it was playing French cricket that also taught him where the batsman's blind spot is. In his words, it is 'on the leg stump, just over the left shoulder of a right-hander, and down round about the place where the batsman is not quite certain whether he should play forward or back'. In big time cricket, O'Reilly relentlessly attacked the batsman's blind spot, making it as difficult as possible for the batsman to survive and score runs.

While O'Reilly was devastatingly effective, there was nothing classical about his action. He looked like a big, bustling bloke from the bush who'd taught himself how to play cricket. Both his grip on the ball and his run-up were unconventional. He bowled leg-spin off 12 paces and his action looked awkward. Jack Fingleton described it as being like 'a kangaroo in the legs and a windmill in the arms'. R.S. Whitington wrote that it '… reminded many of the bunting action of a bull'. While it might have looked unusual, O'Reilly, a champion triple jumper, understood the importance of balance and rhythm in his approach. His method may have been ungainly but he hit the crease with height and momentum.

O'Reilly's grip on the ball had a touch of the bush mechanics to it, and like Bradman's batting grip, people tried to change it when he arrived in the big smoke. When he was 20, O'Reilly went to his first New South Wales practice session. Arthur Mailey, then a selector, suggested he change how he held the ball. Most cricketers placed in such a situation would bow to a higher authority, particularly one who controlled their fate when it came to selections. But that wasn't O'Reilly's style. 'This advice appalled me,' he recalled. 'Here was a man trying to get me to dump all the lessons I had taught myself for nearly ten years. Personal lessons which I learned well enough to find myself in attendance at the nets that afternoon.' He thanked Mailey for his interest but told him he would carry on his way. The same principles that allowed him to develop his own way allowed him to defend it as well. 'I was lucky that all my early family training, inspired by two magnificent parents, had taught me to become wholly self reliant.'

At the end of the training session O'Reilly was approached by a man he later described as a little old joker with a hard-hitter hat and a little white mo. As O'Reilly recalled, he too had some advice: 'He said "I listened to what you had to say to Arthur Mailey, and I'm very proud of you, and you did the right thing." He said "because they tried to do exactly the same thing to me when I came down from Bathurst, they wanted me to change my grip".' The man with the little mo was Charles 'The Terror' Turner who took 101 Test wickets in 17 Tests at the extraordinary average of 16.53. It was something Don Bradman agreed with. He wrote in *Farewell to Cricket*, 'The greatest bowler I ever saw was O'Reilly. His grip was not the kind a coach would have ingrained into a youngster, but thank goodness O'Reilly didn't alter it.' The fact that someone did try to alter his grip, and Bradman's, made O'Reilly contemptuous of cricket coaches. 'I despise coaches,' O'Reilly said in his classic bush vernacular, 'I think coaches do more damage than sudden hail storms.'

So could another O'Reilly emerge from the bush today? Many of Australia's best cricketers still come from country areas. But with saturation television coverage of cricket, it's unlikely a leggie with O'Reilly's unique style would emerge. A young cricketer these days is more likely to copy the style of a player straight off the television. They certainly wouldn't learn how to bowl a wrong 'un by correspondence. There are now enough books, DVDs and spinners kits that show you how to bowl various deliveries. If a player with a strange grip and run-up came through the system today, there's a fair chance one of those coaches that O'Reilly so despised would try and change them.

Wingello remains a cricket-mad town. It seems there are almost as many people playing cricket for Wingello as there are living there. A village of around 200 residents somehow supports three senior teams and four junior teams. They're called, appropriately, the Wingello Tigers and play at the Bill O'Reilly Oval, a bush paddock with an astroturf wicket, a sloping outfield and a magpie who swoops at anyone fielding at deep fine leg. It's a lot different from Bradman Oval, 45 kilometres away in Bowral, which has a turf pitch, a clubhouse, a museum and a statue of the Don.

Wingello Public School has just on 30 students, but they do have better cricket facilities than most. They have their own concrete pitch in the middle of the playground. Boys and girls play on it at playtime and lunch-time all year round. The school is so obsessed with cricket, their school emblem has a set of stumps and a cricket pitch on it. In 2008, a keen young cricketer Matthew Pike won the vote for boy's school captain on the platform of building a new cricket pitch.

Sadly the old gatepost that young Bill worked over outside the family home is no more. The whole house was destroyed by the bushfires that swept through the district in 1965. What a pity. If it was still around today you'd want to put that gatepost on a heritage list and preserve it as a symbol of the bush ingenuity, self-reliance and stubbornness of one of the greats.

Don Bradman

PITCH: Concrete floor outside the laundry.

BAT: Stump.

BALL: Golf ball.

WICKET: Laundry door.

PLAYERS: Don by himself.

RULES: Imaginary field set, if in the air to the fielder, out. If hit through the gap, runs. Bat through Test team 1–11.

HAZARDS: Fast moving ball darting off the tank stand.

BACKYARD DRILLS: Fielding drill with golf ball against the fence.

PLAYERS' COMFORT LEVEL: Intense concentration required, high degree of difficulty.

The most celebrated example of backyard cricket in Australia involved no cricket bat, no cricket ball and no opponents. Don Bradman's improvised childhood game of hitting a golf ball with a stump against the base of a water-tank has become part of cricket folklore. The tale of the batless boy from Bowral ties in nicely with the Aussie battler narrative. But in that primitive game of stump versus golf ball, young Don found advantage, not disadvantage.

In the *Art of Cricket* Bradman suggests the two most important things a young batsmen must learn is to: a) concentrate; and b) watch the ball. You couldn't find a better game to help you concentrate and watch the ball than the tank-stand drill. As he later wrote in *Farewell to Cricket*, 'I can understand how it must have developed the coordination of brain, eye and muscle which was to serve me so well in important matches later on.' Bradman wasn't just good at playing games; he was pretty cluey when it came to inventing them as well.

The game was fast paced. From a few yards away, young Don would throw the golf ball at the brick tank stand and hit it on the rebound. He was dealing with a small, hard, springy ball moving rapidly. His response had to be instinctive. Cricket, like most sports, is a simple game that can become over-complicated. Don was teaching himself to respond in the moment, without his mind being cluttered by thoughts or theories.

There was very little margin for error. Bradman had a thin stump to hit a small ball. He had three curved surfaces to deal with – the golf ball, the stump and the cylindrical brick tank stand. The round surfaces meant the ball could dart at different angles off both the stump and the tank stand, making the 'deliveries' hard to combat and the strokes hard to master. His feet and head had to be in the right place to control his shots. Just hitting the ball was not enough. Bradman played this game in the context of a Test match with 11 imaginary fielders ready to catch any shots in the air.

Young Don would pick his teams based on Test players of the day and work his way through the batting order. The bowling varied according to the nominated players – fast, medium, various forms of spin. Boundaries were judged on how hard the ball was struck. Don kept score in his head. Behind him was a laundry door, which was the wicket. Not only was he trying to hit a small ball with a thin stump, he had the world's largest set of stumps to protect. Playing a normal game of cricket must've seemed comparatively easy.

The game would pass a Productivity Commission inquiry with flying colours. The area was enclosed on three sides, which saved him having to chase the ball on most shots. There were no rain interruptions. The tank stand and laundry area was under cover, so the games could go on for hours. The whole set up was conducive to maximising the number of balls faced before Mum called you in for dinner. You certainly wouldn't face as many rapid-fire deliveries in a schoolyard game or net practice.

While honing his hand–eye coordination and his judgement, the tank-stand drill was also teaching young Don to concentrate. There's no room for drifting off when a golf ball comes flying back at you off a brick cylinder. And there was no breather for him while he waited for the bowler to walk to the top of his mark. This was cricket on fast forward. Don had to be alert, react quickly and watch the ball till the very moment he hit it. It's surprising that a young boy could have the concentration and skill level to play such a difficult game on his own, for so long. It's little wonder he was able to bat and bat and bat when it came to real cricket.

It's no coincidence that Sir Jack Hobbs, the man considered England's greatest ever batsmen and, like Bradman, one of *Wisden*'s five cricketers of the twentieth century, also trained with a stump in his early years. Hobbs's version, though, had a very distinctive British flavour to it. His father was a groundsman at Cambridge University. During school holidays young Jack played against the college servants, facing up to a tennis ball with a stump. They used a tennis net post for a wicket and the pitch was made of gravel. Ah, luxury! Hobbs, like Bradman, was a self-taught cricketer. He played his version of stump cricket when he was around ten years old.

It's not clear how old Don Bradman was when he started playing against the tank stand. The only clue is in the names of the players he pretended to be in those backyard Tests. 'Taylor, Gregory, Collins and so on.' All three made their Test debuts in December 1920, when the first post-war Test was played against England. Two months later, George Bradman took his 12-year-old son to Sydney for his first Test match. After watching Charlie Macartney smash 170 against the English, Don told his father, 'I shall never be satisfied until I play on this ground.'

Is this when Bradman started playing his infamous games against the tank stand? Had he worked out that the best way to become a Test cricketer was to practise hard with the golf ball and stump on his own? Bill O'Reilly once said that even in the cradle Bradman never did anything that wasn't thought out. It does seem peculiar that he played by himself. He wasn't completely isolated like young Richie Benaud in Jugiong. Roland Perry writes in *The Don* that 'Bradman learned early to be at ease with his own company, because there were few mates close to his home.' But as Rodney Cavalier, historian and chairman of the SCG Trust, points out, 'His home was less than one kilometre from the centre of town, only a few hundred metres to Glebe Park where serious cricket was on offer. If Don spent a lot of time alone it was because he chose to.'

While Emily Bradman is said to have bowled to her son in those early days, there are no references in the various Bradman biographies to Don playing backyard cricket with his brother Victor. Victor was only four years older than Don and can't have been completely uninterested in cricket. When Don played his first full season for Bowral Town in 1925/6, his brother was also in the side. Did Don calculate that the solitary path was the best one? That only he could push himself on to bigger and better things? While Bradman, as far as I can tell, was never directly asked this question, he did answer it indirectly: 'In retrospect it was significant, but of course at the time when I was doing it, it had no meaning at all for me other than the fact I was just enjoying myself.'

Not all of Bradman's childhood cricket was played against the tank stand. At school the boys played informal games on a dirt pitch during the lunchbreak. The wicket was the school bell post with a chalk mark to signify the height of the stumps. Bats were of the home-made variety, normally fashioned from gum trees, and shaped like baseball bats. A hard compo ball would crash into the padless limbs of those who played and missed. In his teenage years, Don gained access to two concrete practice wickets, one at his uncle Richard's home, the other at Alf Stephens' place. Alf was the President of the Bowral Town Cricket Club and became a close friend of Bradman.

It should be noted that Don didn't have to play with a stump or a gum tree bat, at least from the age of 13. Sid Cupit, from the Bowral team, gave Don one of his old bats. It had a bit of a crack in it, and Don's father sawed three inches off the bottom of it. 'That bat meant almost everything in the world to me,' Bradman recalled. It now hangs in the Bradman Museum in Bowral. What you find on the back of that bat is instructive. Some of Don's childhood scores are carved on the back of that blade. Even as a boy he had a hunger for runs.

Young Don was always hitting, kicking or throwing some kind of ball. At home he also played tennis against the garage door and would kick a football around the paddock. When walking home from school he threw his golf ball against telegraph poles and tried to catch it off the rebound. All this time he was developing his ball sense. In the *Art of Cricket*, Bradman makes a simple suggestion to young cricketers. 'I would counsel every boy who is interested in batting to play with a ball at every opportunity. Whether it be a golf ball, tennis ball, baseball or any other kind doesn't matter. It will help train the eye and coordinate the brain, eye and muscle.'

Mucking around with a golf ball undoubtedly helped develop Don's fielding. In 1928, when the MCC were playing New South Wales, Bradman ran Wally Hammond out for 225. Back in the dressing room a shocked Hammond asked Patsy Hendren who'd fired the ball in so fast. Hendren replied that it was Bradman, 'He always throws like that. There's no better fielder in this country.' As a boy he would peg the golf ball against a rail that was part of a dividing fence with the neighbour's property. If it hit the rail, it flew back providing a catch. If it hit the palings, he had to chase it. Young Bradman had a strong incentive to learn how to throw accurately.

No cricketer has got near Bradman's achievements with the bat. His Test batting average of 99.94 is nearly forty runs per innings better than his nearest rivals Graeme Pollock, George Headley and Herbert Sutcliffe. He scored a century in 36 per cent of his Test innings. His closest rival on that score is Headley with 25 per cent. Twelve of his 29 Test centuries were converted to double hundreds. Two became triple centuries. No athlete has dominated his or her chosen sport to the same degree as Bradman.

Bradman's phenomenal achievements are an argument against excessive coaching, and in favour of unstructured play. Bradman taught himself how to bat. He did not play a full season of proper structured cricket till he was 17. There was no junior side in Bowral, and there were very few inter-school games in the region. Bradman played only three competition games before leaving school aged 14. (His scores 55 n/o, 115 n/o and 72 n/o.) On Saturdays he acted as Bowral Town's scorer and once as a 13-year-old filled in, scoring 37 n/o and 29 n/o. The tank stand helped him learn how to control his shots and keep his wicket intact. The drill so honed his batting skills that in his first full season of competitive cricket he scored 1317 runs at an average of 94.07, including an innings of 234 against a Wingello attack that included future Test great Bill O'Reilly. By the time Bradman was 18, he was in the New South Wales second eleven. At 19, he was in the New South Wales team. At 20, he was scoring hundreds for Australia.

All of this was done on the back of his unique technique. His grip, stance and stroke play were all considered unorthodox. His top hand was pushed around the back of the handle, allowing him to play the pull shot more readily and keep the ball on the ground. His stance was unusual too, with the bat touching the ground between his feet rather than behind them. His backlift wasn't straight either, moving out towards gully. 'Style?' Bradman once opined, 'I know nothing about style. All I am after is runs.' At one of his first training sessions at the SCG, as a 17-year-old, it was suggested that he might change his grip if he wanted to succeed in the big time. Bradman politely ignored the advice. Even at that young age, Bradman thought his way was the best. And he was right.

Tony Shillinglaw in his book *Bradman Revisited* argues that Bradman's unique style, cultivated in the backyard at Bowral, is what made him better than everyone else. 'Not only did he commence his batting movement before the ball was released, but his unique grip and stance induced a smooth continuous motion of the wrists, arms, shoulders and bat through to the completion of his selected stroke.' Sports scientists have studied this motion and found that it naturally puts you in a position of great balance, on the balls of your feet, ready to move forward or back, giving you more time to get in position to play your shots.

During his playing days, it was thought that it was exceptional eyesight that allowed Bradman to get into position faster to play his shots. Bill Ponsford, the only Australian batsman who rivalled Bradman for heavy scoring in the 1920s and 1930s, said, 'Don sees the ball about two yards sooner than any of the rest of us.' In *The Art of Cricket*, Bradman put this myth to bed. A professor at the University of Adelaide tested his eyes and found Bradman's reaction time was 'minutely slower than that of the average university student'. Shillinglaw's studies suggest it was his technique, evolved out of dealing with the challenge of hitting a golf ball rebounding off a tank stand with a stump, which allowed him to have more time to play shots than other players. Add the concentration skills he learned from the drill, and you have a formidable batsman.

So could a kid growing up in Bowral these days replicate the training methods that made Bradman such a success? Well there are still plenty of decent sized backyards in Bowral, and tank stands are making a comeback thanks to water restrictions and green consciousness. But there's little evidence that Spartan sporting equipment is back in fashion. Keen young cricketers these days seem to have all the latest gear. Today's cricket fans are more likely to be watching it on the television than inventing their own forms of the game. Young Don didn't seem to suffer from that modern day curse of childhood, the low boredom threshold. As Jack Fingleton once said of Bradman, 'He was the only cricketer I knew who never tired of the game.' Perhaps that, mixed in with the golf ball and stump drill, was the secret to his success.

The Hard Road – Depression-era kids and the rise of street cricket

BITUMEN WAS A key ingredient for cricketers who grew up in the Depression. Many of Bradman's 1948 Invincibles, including Sid Barnes, Keith Miller, Ray Lindwall, Neil Harvey and Bill Brown, played much of their early cricket on the road. Street cricket was a cheap form of entertainment and the lack of cars made it possible to have a hit, without being hit.

The 1931 film *That's Cricket* features some choice footage from a street game. A back lane full of barefoot boys with accents as thick as Chips Rafferty's gather around the pitch. There's around six short mid-offs lined up on one side of the fence and six short mid-ons lined up along the other fence. Behind the stumps a sawn-off Wally Grout type figure appears to have his jumper only half on. On closer inspection you realise he's stretched his sleeves over his hands to form a primitive pair of wicket-keeping gloves. He's hemmed in on both sides by slips and leg slips.

When a boy fails to walk, the bowler calls out, 'If you don't get out I'll come and chuck yer out.' The game has a fiercely competitive edge to it. It was this kind of environment that many of the great 1948 side cut their teeth on.

Sid Barnes

PITCH: The streets of Stanmore and a reclaimed rubbish dump.

BAT: Second-hand bats from Sydney University, owned and controlled by Sid.

BALL: Old six stitchers from Sydney University.

WICKET: Telegraph pole or steel pole

PLAYERS: Sid, brother Horrie and boys in the neighbourhood.

RULES: Whatever Sid wanted.

HAZARDS: Cars, trucks and unfriendly neighbours who'd had their windows smashed.

BACKYARD DRILLS: The Bradman stump and golf ball drill. Rehearsing strokes in front of the mirror.

PLAYERS' COMFORT LEVEL: On edge. Police, neighbours and vehicles all posed threats. There was also the risk of gang warfare with neighbouring street teams over dubious umpiring decisions.

Sid Barnes is one of the few Test cricketers to average over 60 with the bat. A member of Bradman's 1948 Invincibles, he was respected by fellow players for his toughness and technique.

Barnes was largely self-taught, learning his craft on the bitumen roads of Sydney's inner west. But cricket wasn't all he learned on the streets. Sid Barnes acquired attitude. He was fearless, supremely confident, and averse to compromise. This cockiness may have helped with his cricket, but it didn't help him get on with cricket administrators. Sid's run-ins with authority ended up cutting short his Test career. But Sid did things his way. Brought up without a father, he learned the art of survival from his mother, a formidable woman who raised three young boys in challenging circumstances.

When Sid Barnes first started playing street cricket in Sydney's inner west in the 1920s, he did so on a professional basis. His eldest brother Horrie, an accountant and cricketer in the local churches competition, paid young Sid to bowl at him after work and on weekends. The brothers set up on the street outside the family home using a telegraph pole for the wicket. The exact location of that street pitch is unclear. At the time the Barnes family moved between two homes in Stanmore, 15 Northumberland Avenue and 105 Corunna Road. Sid was paid sixpence for an hour's worth of trundling and was allowed a bat at the end of each session. The youngest of the three Barnes boys invested his earnings wisely, buying second-hand bats and balls from the Sydney University Cricket Club.

As the sole owner of cricket equipment in a poor neighbourhood where kids were mad for street cricket, Sid had a lot of clout. In the neighbourhood games played in Corunna Road, Sid got two bats to every other kid's one. In his memoir *It Isn't Cricket*, he described his role as being treasurer, financier, organiser and promoter. It's no wonder Sid later butted heads with the administrators in big time cricket; he was used to running the game.

As a boy, Sid already knew a thing or two about the value of money. From the age of seven he collected rent money on behalf of his mother. Making runs and making a buck became his passions. Sometimes he managed to combined both pursuits at once. Prior to the 1948 Lord's Test, Barnes put eight pounds on himself to score a century at odds of 15–1. After getting a duck in the first innings, he came good in the second, scoring 141.

Jane Barnes taught her three sons to be independent and entrepreneurial. Her husband Alf died three months before Sid was born. He contracted typhoid after drinking contaminated water on the family property at Hughenden, in outback Queensland. Soon after Alf's death, the farm and stock were sold, giving the family enough money to move to Sydney and buy a number of houses in the city's inner west. Jane Barnes was a survivor. After Sid was born, she was diagnosed with breast cancer. She told the surgeon to cut off both her breasts to minimise the risk of it coming back.

Life in Stanmore in the 1920s and 1930s was hard, even for those with jobs. Some of the tenants in Jane Barnes's properties could not afford to pay the rent. When Sid was sent to collect the rent, he was told by his mother to get what he could. Even as late as 1937, five years after the Depression reached its nadir, G.R. Gerlach of the Housing Improvement Board described the inner suburbs of Sydney as 'centres of economic waste and breeding places for crime, disease and social demoralisation'. Street cricket in this environment was a cheap form of entertainment for boys with the seat out of their pants.

As Sid played more and more cricket in this tough environment, he continued to improve. Soon he was ready to move up a grade, from Corunna Road to Cardigan Street. The standard was better and so too was the surface. 'Their taxes must've been higher,' Barnes joked. The steel pole they used for a wicket was narrower which meant Sid was less likely to get out. Cardigan Street was where his maternal grandfather George Jeffrey lived. George was a tough nut too. He'd been a coach driver for Cobb and Co. and had been held up a number of times by the notorious bushranger Captain Thunderbolt.

Granddad Jeffrey's sense of calm under fire came in handy. One set of neighbours in Cardigan Street wanted the games of cricket banned after their windows kept getting smashed. 'They were always ringing the police,' Sid recalled in *It Isn't Cricket*, 'and, as far as possible, we tried not to hit the ball in their direction at mid-off. Probably that is why, in my career later, I played the off-drive least of all the strokes.' But not all the kids batted with Sid's discipline. Granddad Jeffrey had his work cut out repairing windows every time a lofted off-drive hit its target.

But Granddad Jeffrey's form of window repair diplomacy was not enough. The local cops would attempt to bust up the kids' games. Sid had to use his wits to outsmart the police. The solution? Shrewd field placements, as Sid revealed in his autobiography, '… we had to post point and square-leg very deep to watch two lanes that led into the main street. The police, naturally, wouldn't come down our main street in a car. They tried to sneak up on us but deep point and square-leg knew their jobs, would whistle when they saw a police-car coming and, moving smartly with bat and ball, we would be over a fence, down the back-garden and "underground" in the sewer in double-quick time. The police never followed us there.'

Despite their success in evading the police, Sid and his mates had to give up on their games in Cardigan Street. Even back in the 1920s, local traffic was becoming a hazard. One day Sid nearly got sideswiped by a truck while running a three. His grandfather suggested they move to a rubbish heap out the back of some of the local houses. Play was adjourned for two weeks while they cleared a section of the tip and cultivated a pitch. Granddad Jeffrey gave them a full kit to compensate them for the move, money he ended up saving in window repairs.

The local boys took to their new pitch with relish. They called themselves The Pit Gang and challenged other boys to matches. Sid knew of another gang of cricket-loving larrikins from his rent collecting, called The Sewer Gang. When they met, the Sewer boys were short on numbers, meaning two of the Pit boys had to umpire. This lead to some contentious decisions. The Sewer boys claimed they were robbed of victory. The game broke up in uproar and threats were exchanged. Sid was later shanghaied in the upper lip by one of the Sewer boys in an act of retribution. He carried the scar for life, a memory of how tough they played cricket in his neighbourhood.

Barnes soon gravitated to formal cricket. He started playing in the Churches competition with his brother and represented New South Wales schoolboys. Petersham invited him to have a run in their third-grade side. But Sid was still very much a boy from the streets and, in what must've been a first for Sydney grade cricket, he went out to bat in a peaked leather cap. While members of The Village People might get away with such headwear, cricketers don't.

Not only did Sid fail to look the part of a cricketer, he committed another faux pas. He padded up and sat in the outer with some of his old cricket mates from the Pit and Sewer games. When a wicket fell, Sid hopped the fence and went out to bat. He touched that cap to acknowledge the cheering from his mates in the crowd, and was promptly bowled for four. When he returned from the crease, he copped a blast from his captain for not entering the ground via the pavilion gate.

Sid played one more game in third-grade, then quit Petersham. He felt out of place and ended up playing in one of his old teacher's teams over the holiday period that summer. Fortunately for Sid they ended up playing a game against Petersham. Dudley Seddon, a New South Wales player who later became an Australian selector, was impressed by Barnes and worked on him to come back to the club. Seddon invited Sid to meet club legend and former Australian player Tommy Andrews. Over a game of billiards they convinced Barnes to give Petersham another go. Sid went back into the lower grades, minus the leather cap, and soon worked his way up to first-grade.

Sid was now determined to make it as a cricketer. He never missed a club practice and three times a week at 5 am, he was down at Petersham Oval running and practising his batting and fielding. His dedication to fitness was legendary and this extra training would pay off. When he shared a record partnership with Bradman in 1946, he was able to bat for 10 hours and 42 minutes in accumulating his 234. Years before this partnership, Bradman had been the inspiration for one of his training routines as a boy in Stanmore – hitting a golf ball with a stump against a wall in his backyard at Northumberland Avenue.

Sid's mother thought he should be concentrating on finding a decent job with career prospects. Male unemployment in the local council area was 32.7 per cent at the time of the 1933 census. Although he ignored his mother's advice on a career, he'd inherited her entrepreneurial flair and determination. Sid got involved in the oil business. He convinced his brother, a professional motorbike rider, to install a petrol pump in the backyard of their house so he could sell petrol to friends, neighbours and fellow cricketers, undercutting the local garage. Sid was able to make money while still dedicating himself to cricket, a skill he turned into an art form later in his career.

At a time when Australian players would struggle to get by, Sid made money out of cricket tours through his business deals. Among his various ventures Sid took table-tennis balls to New Zealand and brought back bolts of cloth from England. Jack Pollard described Sid's selection on one tour as 'a licence to unrestrained trading'. Arthur Morris, his opening partner and roommate on the 1948 tour, had to swap rooms with Ernie Toshack at one stage because all the goods coming and going in the middle of the night were ruining his sleep. *It Isn't Cricket* is unique among cricket autobiographies in that it's as much a catalogue of deals done, and suits bought, as runs scored.

Sid Barnes was a self-made man and a self-taught cricketer. Like O'Reilly, Bradman, and his hero, Stan McCabe, he had little formal coaching. There's no doubt Tommy Andrews and Dudley Seddon had a big influence on his cricket at Petersham, but his personality ensured that he would follow his own path. Sid was encouraged to buy books and study the theories of the game. But in the end he rejected the textbooks and stuck to the style he'd learned on the street and in the Pit. When an ex-international criticised his defence in a Sydney newspaper, Sid bought a full-length mirror and placed it in the backyard so he could check himself out. His defensive stroke looked fine to him. Ray Robinson wrote in an article on Barnes titled *The Artful Dodger*, '… you can see he is a self-made batsman, so full of cricket that handicaps in style could not stop him.' All that ended up stopping Barnes was World War II, which took eight years of Test cricket away from him, and those dreaded cricket officials, who left him out of the Australian team for good in 1951, vetoing the selectors' decision 'on grounds other than cricket ability'.

Modern day cricket has lost much of the individuality of past eras. Centralised coaching means cricketers' techniques have conformed to a norm. Media training teaches elite players to speak in the same uninspiring fashion. Many of them, it seems, visit the same hairdresser who specialises in routine dyed-blonde hairdos. In this environment of conformity it's hard to believe there will ever be another Sid Barnes. He was a one-off even back then.

So what if a young cricketer was growing up in Sid's old haunts of Corunna Road, Northumberland Avenue and Cardigan Street today? Would they be able to play as freely as Sid and his mates did? Northumberland Avenue is now a major thoroughfare for cars travelling between Annandale and Newtown. Playing cricket there would be a suicide mission. Corunna Road is slightly less frantic, but runs down to one of the busiest McDonald's in Sydney. Cardigan Street was getting too dangerous back in the 1920s, and parked cars now block the pitch that Barnes set up across the road out the front of his grandparents' house. Some fancy windows still adorn the Simpsons' old place at Number 22, but they're out of the firing line these days. There's no sign of cricket being played in the neighbourhood streets at all. But if you want to hop the fence and hide from the police in the 'sewers' like Sid and his mates used to do, go ahead. That's one thing about Stanmore that hasn't changed.

Equipment

Jack Fingleton never thought much of young cricketers who had all the latest gear. The former Test cricketer and journalist wrote, '… the petted child with enough equipment to turn out two sides has never yet made any team other than that which stands in need of his gear.' While that comment could not feasibly apply to Sid Barnes, who had both the best kit and the best range of strokes in Stanmore, it is true that many Australian cricketers started off with medieval equipment.

• • •

Richie Benaud's first bat was made from packing-case timber. Stan McCabe's was cut from a lump of wood. Mike Hussey's first blade wasn't even shaped into a bat; it was a piece of spare timber found in the backyard at Mullaloo. Charlie Macartney was given a homemade bat each Christmas, but they'd break soon after due to the lack of a decent handle. Jack Badcock's bats were a little sturdier. His father crafted them from willow grown on the family farm in Tasmania.

• • •

Even balls can be scavenged for next to nothing. Bill O'Reilly bowled a chiselled-down banksia root at his siblings. Stan McCabe's mum made balls from old socks and cork. Arthur Mailey practised his wrong 'un with an orange. Charlie Macartney belted apples. Allan Border found that unripened grapefruits skidded off the concrete strip in his backyard at a ferocious pace. Neil Harvey had to negotiate marbles flying off a concrete strip at a similar speed. Don Bradman whacked golf balls.

• • •

Ball tampering has long been a feature of backyard cricket in Australia. The Waugh brothers taped their balls up to accentuate the swing. Jason Gillespie unfolded a paperclip and taped it down the middle to provide a seam. Colin Miller did the same but with rope. Ray Lindwall, Geoff Lawson and Neil Harvey all wet the ball to make it skid off the hard surface. Jeff Thomson unsurprisingly had to take it further. He lacquered the tennis balls he used against his four brothers in their Bankstown backyard.

• • •

All sorts of objects have been commandeered as stumps. The laundry door worked for Don Bradman, a garage door for the Waugh brothers. Ian Healy used a rubbish bin. Betty Wilson, Keith Miller and Keith Stackpole all batted in front of Melbourne lamp-posts. Alan Davidson placed three gum-tree sticks at the end of his home-made pitch. Glenn McGrath bowled at a 44-gallon drum. Bob Simpson defended a piece of concrete dragged from a nearby quarry. Monty Noble attacked a biscuit tin. Ray Lindwall rattled an old kerosene tin.

• • •

But my favourite piece of cricket equipment comes courtesy of 1948 Invincible, Colin McCool. The leg-spinning all-rounder, like Victor Trumper, went to Crown Street School in Surry Hills. McCool and his mates played in the local streets and on concrete pitches in Moore Park. The boys pooled what limited money they had to buy some cricket equipment. Unfortunately they didn't have enough to buy a pair of wicket-keeping gloves. The solution, as McCool recalled, was an act of ingenuity. 'We bought a pair of leather gardening gloves and smothered the palms with hot bitumen from the melting Sydney roads.'

Keith Miller

PITCH: In the street and the lawn in the backyard.

BAT: Cut-down bat

BALL: Tennis ball

WICKET: Lamp-post

PLAYERS: Keith, brothers Ray and Les Junior, father Les Senior, neighbours and Buttons the dog.

RULES: Six and out.

HAZARDS: Ball thief living next door.

BACKYARD DRILLS: Ball in stocking.

PLAYERS' COMFORT LEVEL: Enjoyable despite Horrie the cranky neighbour.

Even from a young age, Keith Miller knew how to clear a fence. Playing in his backyard in Melbourne in the 1920s and 1930s, he regularly belted tennis balls into his neighbour's back garden. Miller went on to thrill cricket fans across the world with his powerful stroke play. Batting for the Dominions XI at Lord's in 1945, he slugged seven sixes, including one that landed on the roof of the broadcasting box. Former English Test cricketer Sir Pelham Warner reckoned it was the greatest display of hitting he'd seen in 60 years of watching cricket. But before Miller became the hero of Lord's, he had to deal with someone who wasn't so appreciative of his six-hitting ability.

Horrie Parsons lived next door to the Miller family in Denver Crescent, Elsternwick. An alert neighbour, he seemed particularly sensitive to the sounds of boys playing cricket. If Keith hit a ball over the fence, Parsons would seize it with all the efficiency of a Wimbledon ball boy. 'He was brilliant in his way,' Keith recalled in *The Golden Nugget*, 'for sometimes he would be out and on to the ball before it had stopped bouncing. He was ruthless, too, for he kept all the balls. I reckon he must have collected hundreds of them.' It turned out that Parsons was feeding the stray balls to Bill and John Hosking, a couple of tennis-playing boys who lived across the road.

Before Keith learned of the joys of hitting over the top, he was schooled in the importance of a good defence and a solid technique. The youngest of four siblings, he had two elder brothers and a father to teach him the fundamentals of the game. 'I grew up in an atmosphere of cricket,' Miller wrote. His brothers, Ray and Les Junior, played cricket for Brighton Footballers. They recognised from an early age that Keith had extraordinary ability and would wake him up early before school to practise with him. 'They weren't very good players, but I think they were very good teachers,' Keith recalled. Les Miller Senior was adamant a young boy should learn how to bat facing a tennis ball. That way he would get in behind the ball without worrying about being hit.

Keith first picked up a bat in the backyard of a terrace house in Benjamin Street, Sunshine, in Melbourne's west. His father Les was an engineer with H.V. McKay, the company that produced the Sunshine Harvester, which gave the suburb its name. A successful bush footballer in the wheat-belt town of Warracknabeal, he moved to Sunshine when H.V. McKay moved their operations there. When Keith was around six or seven, the family moved to Elsternwick, 9 kilometres south-east of the centre of Melbourne. The new neighbourhood was a good place to get a game. In nearby Brentani Avenue, the local kids played Test matches until dark using a lamp-post as a wicket.

Norma Ward, who still lives in Denver Crescent, says the street games were fairly one-sided. 'Keith would bowl to us, and get us all out. Then he'd get in and all the boys and I had to run all over the street chasing the ball. He was a good sportsman.' If Keith couldn't get a game in the neighbourhood or with his brothers, he played alone in his backyard. He'd 'beg, borrow or steal' his sister's stockings, place a ball in them and tie it to the clothesline. He'd hit the ball in the stocking for hours, developing his reflexes and concentration.

The repetitious thud of young Miller's cut-down bat hitting the ball in the stocking drove his ball-poaching next-door neighbour batty. When it was suggested he practise somewhere else, Keith held his ground. 'If the fellow on one side of our house could rev up a motorbike at some sleeping hour every morning, and the neighbours on the other side could pinch all the cricket balls when the stockings gave way, I certainly was not going to stop my harmless little bit of recreation,' Miller said 50 years later. 'Perhaps those were the first seeds of the self-reliance, or plain cussedness, which helped build my character.'

Miller's boyhood hero was the Victorian run machine Bill Ponsford. The first batsman to twice score over 400 in an innings, Ponsford was at his peak when Miller was seven years old. In just four first-class innings in 1927/8 he scored a phenomenal 1013 runs. Les Miller Senior took his children to the MCG and implored them to watch Ponsford. Watching Ponsford became a bit of an obsession for young Keith. If he wasn't at the MCG, he simply walked down the road. The record-breaking batsman lived just 400 metres away in Orrong Road, Elsternwick. Miller wrote 'I would often walk past his house just in the hope of catching a glimpse of the great man.'

Having a Test cricketer in the neighbourhood can act as a spur to a young player. Ian Redpath, who grew up four doors down from Lindsay Hassett's old home in Geelong, wrote that it made him 'aware that it was possible to reach the top'. Vic Richardson spent his early years in a house across the road from Australian captain Joe Darling. Charlie Macartney ended up practising with Victor Trumper, when his hero moved in nearby. Ray Lindwall tried to impress his neighbour, Bill O'Reilly, when the great leg-spinner walked past their street cricket games on his way home from work. When Ponsford moved out of the neighbourhood, Miller didn't stop stalking his hero. His sister Gladys married and relocated to Glenhuntly, the same suburb Ponsford had moved into. 'My sister was astonished at the number of visits I paid her,' Miller wrote. 'I am afraid it was not due to any increase in brotherly affection – I just wanted to see "Ponny"'.

Ponsford continued to be an inspiration to young Miller. 'I idolised this man and I tried to build my game on him.' Ponsford was a good choice for a role model. When Keith Miller was at his peak, he was 185 centimetres tall, broad-shouldered and built like a full-forward. But as a 15-year-old boy, he was under 150 centimetres and built more like a jockey. His brothers called him 'Weedy'. Because of his lack of size, he struggled to hit the ball with the same power as his peers. By idolising a batsman whose game was based on defence and accumulation, Miller had picked the perfect model for a small boy to emulate.

Initially Keith's size was held against him. He trained hard with St Kilda, but they refused to pick him, even in their fifth-grade side. One club member bailed him up and said, 'Do you know what's wrong with you? You're too small for playing cricket, you're too small.' The boy, who went on to terrorise Len Hutton and other opening batsmen with his brisk bouncers, was considered so impotent with the ball that he was kicked out of the practice nets. Heck Oakley, a Victorian Shield player, told Miller to 'take that ball and hand it to someone who can bowl'.

But Hughie Carroll, a coach who'd been giving Keith and other players lessons on a backyard wicket in Elsternwick, recognised Keith's potential. Carroll suggested he come and play for his club South Melbourne. They immediately picked him in first-grade, thus preventing St Kilda from reclaiming Miller as a local player later on. At the age of 15, and armed with a cut-down bat, Keith made his district cricket debut.

In the last match of the season against Carlton, he came up against his schoolmaster at Melbourne High, former Australian captain Bill Woodfull. Carlton ripped through South Melbourne's top order and Miller came to the crease at 6 for 32. He batted for two and a half hours and made 61. *The Herald*'s match report described him as 'A Ponsford in miniature'. Watching Ponsford had paid off. He soon grew around 30 centimetres in a period of 12 to 18 months. With size came power and he was able to combine the technique of Ponsford with the strength of Jack Gregory.

In 1999, Keith acknowledged the significance of those backyard training sessions in developing his cricket. He wrote the following letter to his brother Ray:

Ray, thanks to you, Les and Dad, cricket has given me a most interesting life.

The places I've been to, the people I've met is [sic] unbelievable, all because of my cricket exploits.

And it's all because of the endless hours, you, Les and Dad taught me in the backyard.

So this letter is to say thank you.

It's [sic] a sort of letter I should've been writing when Les and Dad was [sic] around, but like many things 'I'll do it tomorrow' style which never gets done.

So Ray, I finally made it. All my cricket was due to the three of you – nobody else.

My most genuine thanks Ray.

Pop –Weedy [family nicknames]

Ray's daughter Jan rang Keith after her father received the letter. She wanted to thank him and tell him how much it meant to Ray. Keith said he didn't want anyone else taking any credit for his success in cricket. It was all down to them. Ray Miller died later that year.

So what of a young cricketer in the Miller mould growing up in Elsternwick today? Brentani Avenue remains a cul-de-sac, so you could still have a hit there, and Keith's old backyard is not that different to what it was in the 1930s. Norma Ward says she doesn't see or hear cricket played by children in the neighbourhood any more.

One's thing's for sure. You'd be hard pressed to find a first-class cricketer with the attitude of Keith Miller in the professional age. His perspective on cricket, that it was a game that should be played for enjoyment, was very much a product of his war-time experiences. Miller flew Mosquito fighter planes over Germany in World War II. He saw many of his mates killed, and narrowly avoided death on a number of occasions. When asked about the pressures of playing cricket he said, 'Pressure, I'll tell you what pressure is. Pressure is a Messerschmitt up your arse, playing cricket is not.' Now there's a sentence you're unlikely to hear uttered by a modern day cricketer.

Ray Lindwall

PITCH: Bitumen pitch on Hudson Street, and dirt pitch in the backyard.

BAT: Conventional cricket bat.

BALL: Tennis ball in street, compo ball in backyard.

WICKET: Kerosene tin or butter box on the street, stumps in the backyard.

PLAYERS: Ray, his brother Jack, and boys from the neighbourhood.

RULES: Six and out.

HAZARDS: Mrs Chambers' dive-bombing pet magpie and a cranky neighbour known as Judge Jeffries.

BACKYARD DRILLS: Bowling stones at fences, posts and lamp-posts.

PLAYERS' COMFORT LEVEL: Intensely competitive matches against older boys.

While Keith Miller was learning on the lawn at Elsternwick, his future Test partner in pace was bowling on bitumen. Ray Lindwall started out playing in the street in Sydney. It wasn't just any street, either. Lindwall lived in Hudson Street, Hurstville, the same street as 'Tiger' Bill O'Reilly, who was at that stage leading Australia's bowling attack. Ray, his brother and their mates used to compete to get the Tiger's attention as he walked home from his teaching job at Kogarah High.

Just as the sly grog shops of the day employed cockatoos to look out for the cops, Lindwall and his mates would send someone down to the street corner so they knew when O'Reilly was coming. 'Look out, here comes the Tiger!' are the first words of Lindwall's autobiography, as he recalls the rallying cry for the Hudson Street boys. If Lindwall was bowling he added an extra few yards to his run up and tried to knock over the kerosene tin or butter box they were using as a wicket. There's a good chance he would've hit it too. In his Test career, Lindwall was to take 228 wickets – 45 per cent of them bowled. *Flying Stumps* was appropriately the name of that autobiography.

If Bill O'Reilly was paying any attention to the Flying Kero Tins, he didn't let on. He had his head buried in the afternoon tabloid as he strolled home past the young cricketers so desperate for his attention. Lindwall was sure O'Reilly was ignoring them, even though the games had been set up strategically along the Tiger's path home.

But O'Reilly not only had a shrewd cricket brain, as a teacher he was used to surreptitiously monitoring schoolkids. He could pick apart a young cricketer's strengths and weaknesses out of the corner of his eye while reading the sports pages. Picked for St George's first-grade side as a sixteen-year-old, Lindwall asked his captain if he remembered him from Hudson Street. 'I remember you alright,' O'Reilly said. 'You were the grubby kid with the ridiculously long run. You looked a bit useful in spite of that. Let's see if you have come on at all.'

Lindwall was soon training down at the Hurstville nets with

the other St George players from 6 am. O'Reilly was concerned about the lack of adequate practice in the afternoon sessions and ordered twice-weekly morning sessions. While this might have appalled others, Lindwall was already prepared for the Tiger's unorthodoxy. As a child, he and his brother Jack rose at 6 am so they could have a game on the dirt wicket in their backyard. After a quick breakfast it was off to school for more cricket and back home for another game on the street. On the weekends they found games at local parks. As Lindwall wrote, 'Cricket mad? Of course we were, but I believe that 99 out of every 100 who rise above the common level in ball games have laid the foundations by a similar "lunacy" in the schoolboy days.'

It was through this 'lunacy' that Lindwall was learning, by repetition, the skills of cricket. Even during the football season, Lindwall continued practising his run up and delivery stride. If he couldn't find someone to bowl at in Hudson Street, he bowled stones at lamp-posts, trees, or fences. Even while serving with the army in New Guinea he would mark out 22 yards and bowl pebbles at a post or tree, sometimes for hours on end. '… this pebble bowling helped me to keep thinking of cricket,' Lindwall wrote, 'and I have no doubt that the constant bowling was good for developing accuracy.' It was his accuracy that stood Lindwall apart from other fast men. Denis Compton thought he was the greatest 'controlled' fast bowler he saw. Fred Trueman considered him 'the king' of fast bowlers describing him as 'a quick bowler with the accuracy of a medium pacer'. Alec Bedser said, 'I've never seen anyone as fast having such control as he had.' He could not only bowl fast and accurately, he could swing the ball both ways.

For cricketers of the pre-television era, the first big match they went to often had a big influence on them. After seeing his first

Test match in 1921, Don Bradman vowed to his father he would not be satisfied until he played on the SCG. A Clarrie Grimmett six-wicket haul inspired a nine-year-old Richie Benaud on his first trip to the SCG. In December 1932, Ray and Jack Lindwall headed off to the first Test of the Bodyline series. From their spot on the hill they marvelled at Stan McCabe's brilliant 187 not out. But English fast bowler Harold Larwood, who took ten wickets for the match, also caught Ray's eye. 'I noticed his rhythm and consciously tried to copy it,' Lindwall wrote. By the time he made his Test debut, comparisons between the two were already being made.

As a young boy, Ray Lindwall had to rely on neighbourhood games to quench his appetite for cricket. His primary school, St Mary's Star of the Sea, did not have organised sport. Fortunately he had his elder brother Jack to play against. Jack and Ray's backyard Tests were played with a compo ball. As at Lord's, if you scored a century your name was etched on the honour board – except at Hudson Street it was in pencil on a sheet of tin near the shed.

Over the fence into Mrs Chambers' place was 'six and out', and with good reason. Their next-door neighbour had a pet magpie tied to a long chain that dive-bombed any young boys on a retrieval mission. Ray attributed his strong off-side game to the bird over the fence at deep square leg. The magpie did meet an untimely end when a shot cleared the fence. One of Ray's mates went to retrieve the ball armed with a stump for self-defence. The magpie swooped, the boy's cross-bat swing connected, and Ray from then on could play on-side strokes with more safety.

These backyard and street games were critical in teaching Ray how to compete. Jack Lindwall and his mates were two to three years older and Ray tested himself against boys who were bigger, stronger and more experienced. At the age of seven, Ray was allowed to play in their Test matches. The Hudson Street boys would challenge the boys from The Avenue. The games were intense. Even getting selected in the street teams was a competitive process.

Ray's brother Jack was a fine athlete who according to Ray, 'could play cricket better than any boy in the Hurstville district'. Jack didn't push on with his cricket but went on to score over a 100 tries for St George in first-grade rugby league. Playing tough cricket against his brother and other older boys meant that when it came to playing in his own age group, Ray dominated. One morning he hit 219 in just 75 minutes for Oatley Juniors. Just to prove he could mix it with the men, he rode his bike to Cronulla with his kit on his handlebars and peeled off an unbeaten century for the Carlton Waratahs.

Lindwall scored two Test centuries but according to Keith Miller, Ray considered a 70-odd not out he made playing in the streets in Hurstville to be his best knock. As Miller recounted, 'Hits over the fence counted six and out, runs did not count behind the kerosene tin which served for a wicket, and there were more than 50 kids fielding. Ray must have had to spank the ball pretty hard on the drive to elude that mob, but only darkness stopped his knock.'

It's hard to imagine 50 kids playing street cricket anywhere in Sydney now and it certainly wouldn't happen in Hudson Street. The street outside the Lindwalls' old place now has a speed hump to slow the traffic. When I went to check out the old house at number 57, I was hoping I'd hear the cries of 'Howzat!' from the backyard where Ray and Jack used to play. Sadly that house and Mrs Chambers' house have been knocked down, and replaced by a block of flats that overlaps the two properties. Hudson Street is now lined with units, maximising rental returns but minimising room for play. The street does have a park, but the afternoon I visited, no one was playing sport there.

St George is still producing good cricketers. The Saints won four out of five Poidevin Gray (under 21) championships contested between 2003 and 2008 and won back-to-back first-grade premierships in 2007/08 and 2008/9. One of their best, New South Wales all-rounder Moises Henriques, grew up in the area but struggled to find kids in the neighbourhood to play cricket with. He ended up playing alone in the backyard, throwing a ball against the wall, trying to hit it past tables and chairs that acted as fielders.

Warren Saunders, a former Shield player and a patron of the St George club, is not surprised Henriques struggled to get a hit. 'There's not as many pick up games,' Saunders says. 'It's all structured, it's all organised.' Saunders grew up playing on a rolled mud pitch on a vacant block in Bexley in the 1940s. Out of those games came one of Australia's finest stroke players, Norm O'Neill, and the beginnings of a junior club, the Bexley Dragons. That vacant block, like Ray Lindwall's old house, has been turned into units. In the St George area, the backyards are being built out, open space is evaporating and the streets are just too busy. The conditions that cultivated the likes of Lindwall and O'Neill are gone forever.

Betty Wilson

PITCH: Street.

BAT: Cricket bat.

BALL: Tennis ball.

WICKET: Lamp-post.

PLAYERS: Betty, brother George and neighbourhood kids.

RULES: Conventional cricket rules.

BACKYARD DRILLS: Ball in the stocking drill. Throwing rocks at lamp-posts.

PLAYERS' COMFORT LEVEL: Tough. Like anything in Collingwood during the Depression.

If you were taking only averages into account, Betty Wilson would have to rate as the most dominant all-rounder in the history of international cricket. None of the greats, not Sobers, Miller, Botham, nor Imran Khan, could beat Betty's figures. In Test matches she averaged 57.46 with the bat, 11.8 with the ball. In her first Test she scored 90 and took ten wickets. In her second

Test she scored a hundred and took nine more scalps. She was the first woman to take a Test hat-trick, the first cricketer, male or female, to score a century and take over ten wickets in the one Test. Her best Test bowling figures were 7/7.

From a young age, Betty was playing against older boys in a competitive environment. 'She was the only girl in the street who played street cricket,' her elder brother George recalls. 'She played football too, and she could kick a ball as well as I could.' George was no mug with the boot. He played for Collingwood as a fullback. The Wilsons spent their early years in Maugie Street, Abbotsford, just around the corner from Victoria Park, Collingwood's legendary home ground. Their father George Senior was a trainer with the football club and worked as a bootmaker in Hoddle Street.

Betty was about to turn eight when the Great Depression hit. Over 30 per cent of the men in the Collingwood district became unemployed. Children scrounged scraps of leather off Hoddle Street bootmakers like George Wilson. They called it 'Collingwood coke' and took it home to burn for heating and cooking. Street cricket was the ideal form of entertainment for kids from such impoverished homes. All you needed was a piece of wood, a ball and a competitive streak. Betty defended her wicket, an old wooden lamp-post in Maugie Street, with the kind of determination that later saw her dominate women's cricket. 'She didn't go out first ball, that's for sure,' says George Wilson, 'and she could bowl as well as the boys.'

When Betty was about ten, her family moved to Hodgkinson Street, Clifton Hill, less than a kilometre away. It was here that her cricketing talents were first spotted. One night she went for a stroll with her father up to Mayor's Park, where the Collingwood women's team practised. When a ball was hit through the fence,

Betty picked it up and hurled it back to the wicketkeeper with a strong arm already honed from her street games. As the balls kept coming, Betty kept pinging them back. By the end of the practice session, two club members approached her and asked if she'd like to play. 'I asked Dad, "Can I?"' Betty recalled. 'He said, "If you want to." That would be Thursday night training, and Saturday I was playing with them.'

Betty's first season was no dream debut. In one of her first matches she was hit in the stomach while batting. Some members of the community thought it was too dangerous for a ten-year-old to be playing with adults. The issue was even raised at local council level. But Betty's parents were adamant she should be allowed to play. 'She has been hit once,' they said. 'She won't be hit again.' Betty, with a little help from her father, went to work on a Bradmanesque backyard batting drill. George Wilson didn't know much about cricket but he came up with the idea of putting an old cricket ball in a stocking and hanging it over the wire clothesline. If Betty kept hitting the ball it would get her feet moving; if she moved her feet correctly she was less likely to be hit.

The drill didn't just help with self-preservation. It was beneficial to Betty's all-round game. 'Whichever shots you played you had to quickly reverse into the batting stance,' Betty recalled. 'If you played a cover drive it's going to come back to you on the on-side so you had to glance at that, and then it would come back to you for a late cut. You could raise it so you could teach yourself how to dodge a fast ball or to hook or cut. You could drop it down and practise playing yorkers.' After watching Lindsay Hassett play the late cut at the MCG one day, she came home and practised it on the clothesline. The backyard drill, like Bradman's golf ball and stump game, was the perfect way to work on footwork and hand–eye coordination. Betty did it for hours at a time.

While her peers practised once a week, Betty tried to practise every day. Because of the fast paced nature of the stocking drill, she faced many more deliveries than her team-mates did at club practice. The drill was always conducted in full kit, to replicate match conditions. Before she pulled out one of her mum's old lisle stockings and flung it around the clothesline, she always put on her cricket boots, pads and gloves. Betty continued with this ritual right up until she retired from Test match cricket at the age of 38, and believes it contributed significantly to her success. 'I think this was probably why I may have been just a little bit better than a lot of other people.'

Another all-rounder of note growing up in 1930s Melbourne found the drill to be beneficial. At the same time Betty Wilson was borrowing her mum's cotton stockings, 12 kilometres away in Elsternwick, a young Keith Miller was pinching his sister's hosiery for the same purpose. Forty-odd years later, Steve Waugh threw one of his mum's stockings over a beam in the garage of the family home and started working away on his technique. Waugh credits the 'thousands of hours' he spent hitting a ball in a stocking to helping to develop his patience, perseverance and straight bat.

Betty's appetite for practice was not limited to batting. She would go down to the local nets and practise her spin-bowling by placing pieces of cotton wool on the pitch at the point she was aiming for. She used two pieces of cotton wool. One for a good length ball to a tall batter, and one for a shorter opponent. 'I'm sure that's how I got so many wickets.' Wilson said 'Through being accurate and making people reach for the ball, by keeping it just short of their reaching ability.' Because she was so accurate she hit the target regularly at practice. Through trial and error she worked out that coins and other targets would move once hit, but cotton wool stayed put. Up until her death in January 2010 she used the same technique to practise her lawn bowls.

As a fielder Betty also stood out from her peers. She was fast across the ground and had an arm like a baseballer. While playing at the MCG in 1949, Betty amazed the crowd by throwing the ball all the way from the boundary to the wicketkeeper. To do that on the world's largest Test cricket field was an impressive effort, something many male players struggle to achieve. Betty worked on her arm by throwing stones at lamp-posts in the streets of Collingwood. 'My dad used to say you can throw anything anywhere as long as you can see where it's going to land.' To work on her ground fielding she ran through paddocks, bending on the fly to pick the tops off daisies before throwing them towards an imaginary wicketkeeper.

While street cricket is virtually impossible in Melbourne these days, the stocking drill can be played pretty much anywhere where there's a clothesline, tree branch or beam. Up until her death Betty hung onto one of her mum's old stockings in the garage at home, just in case. After she retired she coached a girls' team and tried to convince them that it was the perfect way to train. 'They all laughed at me,' Betty says. 'They just thought it was silly.' But not everyone does. A sports company in Adelaide now retails a product called Eye-In that's like a combination between Don Bradman's golf ball and stump routine and Betty Wilson's stocking drill. If hitting a ball in the backyard repetitively by yourself worked for Australia's greatest ever male and female cricket players, you'd think it might be worth having a look at.

Neil Harvey

PITCH: Cobblestone lane in Fitzroy.

BALL: Tennis ball, often wet.

BAT: Normal bat.

PLAYERS: Neil, and his brothers Merv, Mick, Harold, Ray and Brian, and any neighbours game to play.

RULES: Out if caught on the full off the walls, two runs for hitting the gutter, four for the fence, six for over the fence. Game over if through neighbour's window.

HAZARDS: A window at straight hit.

BACKYARD DRILLS: Marble cricket on a short pitch on the concrete in the backyard.

PLAYERS' COMFORT LEVEL: Tight crammed spaces, pitch a minefield, ultra-competitive brothers.

In an age of flat tracks, fat bats and short boundary ropes, a cricket fan can crave a pitch with a bit of life in it. In inner-city Melbourne lies one such deck. It takes vicious cut and variable bounce. But while a pitch like this might improve the self-esteem of underperforming bowlers, it can also cultivate quality batsmen. The pitch, an old cobblestone lane off Argyle Street, Fitzroy, is where Neil Harvey and his five brothers learned how to play cricket.

In this era of drop-in pitches perhaps Cricket Australia should dig up the old laneway and transfer it to their Centre for Excellence. If you could survive on this dodgy deck, with a wet tennis ball darting off the bluestone on a good length, you could score runs anywhere. All six Harvey boys, Merv, Mick, Harold, Ray, Neil and Brian, prospered when they moved onto turf wickets. All played first-grade for Fitzroy as batsmen. Four of them scored first-class centuries. Two of the brothers played for Australia. Merv opened the batting in one Test; Neil became one of Australia's greatest ever batsmen, touring with Bradman's 'Invincibles' as a 19-year-old, and being selected in Australia's team of the twentieth century.

The area the Harvey boys grew up in was a little like that bluestone pitch – rough around the edges and difficult to negotiate. During the 1930s Fitzroy was an industrial suburb short on industry. Unemployment rates were among the highest in Melbourne. The infant mortality rate was the worst in the state. In 1933, five years after Neil Harvey was born, Father Gerard Tucker set up the Brotherhood of St Laurence in Fitzroy, declaring a 'War on Slums'. The Harvey family, Elsie, Horace, their six boys and daughter, Rita, kept their heads above water in a rented house at 198 Argyle Street, out the back of the Lifesavers confectionery factory where Horace held onto a job as a caretaker and processor. All six boys shared the one room.

Father Tucker used to say that if Christ were to come to Melbourne 'He would begin His work in the streets and lanes of Fitzroy'. The Anglican priest would probably have approved of the Harvey boys' laneway Test matches played on Sundays. There was much worse going on in Fitzroy's streets at the time. Besides, the games only began after the boys had attended Sunday school. Other boys in the neighbourhood keen for a game would also turn up. Among them were Allan Ruthven and Harold Shillinglaw, who both went on to play first-grade football for Fitzroy; Ruthven became a Hall of Famer, while Shillinglaw also represented Victoria in cricket.

An old kerosene tin was used as the wicket. A tennis ball was the missile of choice, dipped in water so it would skid off the cobblestones. A gutter ran down the middle of the pitch, which was around 3 metres wide. Walls on either side cut the pitch off in a claustrophobic fashion, but then six brothers who shared a room were used to working well in tight spaces. The batsmen had to be precise with their shots. There weren't too many gaps in the field. You ran when you could and got two runs for hitting the kerb at the end of the lane. If you hit the fence across the road, it was four, over it was six. A straight drive hit crisply could make it into Argyle Street where a nearby window was smashed 'quite a few times' as Neil recalls.

Maybe it was Horace Harvey who brought in the rule that you could get caught on the full off the walls. With Dad having to fork out for broken windows in financially difficult times, there needed to be an incentive for the boys to keep the ball along the ground. Stumps were invariably called if the window was smashed. To this day, behind the bowler's run-up, there's a window there, and you can imagine the young Harvey boys eyeing it off.

Throughout Neil Harvey's Test career, he had a reputation for immaculate footwork. Richie Benaud said of his former team mate, 'He was the most difficult batsman to bowl to. He would dance down the wicket to balls that an ordinary batsman would have played defensively.' But amazingly, despite his desire to get down to the pitch of the ball, Harvey was never stumped in any of his 137 Test match innings. He believes those games he played as a youngster, where the ball deviated sharply off the cobblestones, helped get his feet moving. 'The ball did all sorts of funny things – both height and sideways movement – and it made you put your feet in the right place, and my idea of batting is that if your feet are in the right place, you've got a hell of a good chance of winning.'

Neil Harvey first started training with Fitzroy Cricket Club as a 12-year-old. Former Victorian off-spinner Joe Plant immediately recognised his potential. Plant designed a batting drill that further improved Neil's footwork. He marked a spot on the pitch and got Harvey to rush down the wicket to that point. No ball was used. Once Plant was satisfied his feet were moving properly, they had a proper net, with Plant tossing up his off-spinners, encouraging young Neil to get down the pitch and hit him.

The combination of repetitive play on the cobblestones, and the unorthodox coaching methods of Joe Plant had Harvey's feet moving sharply and instinctively. Neville Cardus, an English writer and critic, later referred to him as the 'Cavalier on Swift Feet'. As Cardus saw it, Harvey rarely got out due to poor technique. 'Harvey has seldom lost his wicket to a technically bad stroke; he has lost it, more often than not, to the wrong technically *right* stroke. In other words he has fallen because of an error of judgement – not an error of technique or style.'

Neil Harvey saved many of his best Test match innings for difficult pitches. While he failed in Jim Laker's Test of 1956, bagging a pair on a crook pitch, he was known for playing the big innings when others were struggling. In 1950, he scored 151 not out as Australia successfully chased 336 on a sticky wicket in South Africa. Richie Benaud described his 96 on matting in Pakistan in 1959, when he was battling dysentery, a tricky pitch and Fazal Mahmood as 'the best I ever saw from him'. He played a lone hand of 92 not out as Australia fell to the pace of a fired-up Frank Tyson on a Sydney greentop in 1954. Harvey is adamant that playing on the cobblestones as a young boy helped him tough it out on difficult pitches later in his career. 'It was a great learning experience to play on something like that and it was something that you can learn technique from, which I think the blokes of today lack something of.'

Everything about Neil Harvey's cricket career was accelerated. Dragged along in the slipstream of his competitive elder brothers, he was playing district cricket for Fitzroy at 13. By the time he was 15, he was in their first eleven, competing against state and Test players. He debuted for Victoria at 18 while still an apprentice fitter and turner, and played his first Test match as a 19-year-old. He scored his first Test hundred in just his second match. As the sixth of seven children he learned to compete against older, stronger siblings who were already playing against men. 'I'm quite convinced that playing with brothers that were better than I was at that age did a lot to foster my cricket career later in life,' Harvey says.

In a tough era, in a tough neighbourhood, it's hard to imagine the elder Harvey brothers going easy on young Neil. One of the games they invented, like Bradman's tank stand game in the backyard at Bowral, did much to improve the reflexes of a future Test great. One day Neil came home from school to find his brothers playing a game on the concrete strip in the backyard. They were using a marble for a ball, and a home-made cut-down bat. The marble was bowled from half a pitch length away and zinged off the concrete. The first ball young Neil faced cracked him on his gloveless knuckles. 'I thought what's going on here! I just wasn't used to the pace or the bounce of the glass marble flying off the concrete. But I tell you what; it sharpens your reflexes after a little short stint of that. I think that was one of the other things apart from the cobblestone lane which helped me, especially with footwork and picking up the ball quickly. I think they are two of the great assets of playing the game. Bradman's main asset was picking the ball up quicker than anybody else, and his movement of foot.'

When the Harvey brothers played their version of 'marbles', they made sure they had a couple of fielders perched close in to the bat. It sounds not unlike the kind of game a young Douglas Jardine might have played, plotting future Bodyline tactics in the schoolyard at Winchester College. It would have no doubt toughened the boys up, as well as improving their reflexes, and getting them used to short-pitched bowling. Merv Harvey was renowned for his hook shot. Ray Robinson wrote of Neil Harvey's ability to handle the short stuff, 'He was the coolest receiver of bouncers I ever saw. No back-pedalling or ducking. Neil swayed his head across just enough to allow the rearing ball to hiss past his right shoulder.'

Neil Harvey's attitude to batting was not unlike that of Trumper and Macartney. All three were fiercely competitive and wanted to win. But they weren't paralysed by fear or full of angst about the consequences of a poorly judged shot. They all gave the ball a whack and played shots to balls others wouldn't dream of trying to score off. Len Hutton, a batsman obsessed with survival, once said to Neil, 'You play and miss too many balls.' Harvey replied, 'I have a go at 'em anyway.' Harvey had this attitude from early on in his career. In his first Test against

England, with Australia facing the potential of following on, he strode to the crease and said to his partner Keith Miller, 'What's going on out here? Let's get stuck into them, eh?' Harvey made 112 off 183 balls using his feet sublimely to deal with the turn of Jim Laker. Neville Cardus wrote he 'played less by calculation than joyous impulse'.

Perhaps this lack of fear came from Neil's father, Horace. As Melbourne journalist Percy Beames put it, 'Their father strongly discouraged post-mortems if one of his sons had lost his wicket without scoring. He knew that pondering over failure was bad for morale. Neil Harvey gave credit to his father's low-key nature. 'Dad never once tried to advise us how to bat. This was a good thing as I have always felt that a too enthusiastic parent can quite easily wreck the progress of a good young player. I've seen it happen quite a few times when a father has thought himself much more talented than his son, tried to tell him how he thought the game should be played, and ended up ruining his son's future. That's why I give full credit to my father who would say: "Well done" when either of us made a few runs, or just: "Bad luck – get them next time" when we missed out.'

Horace Harvey did his boys a few favours it seems. Moving into a place with a cobblestone lane down the side may have been one of the best of them. It certainly honed the skills of six talented boys who had a love for cricket. Sadly, street cricket is no longer played in that old laneway. There's not even a plaque to commemorate the significance of the games played there in the 1930s and 1940s. The Harveys' old home at 198 Argyle Street was knocked down and converted into offices. The lane, once public property, is now owned by a group of property developers. The famous pitch is now locked off by a grey B&D roller door.

The Radio Age –
Synthetic tests make
backyard tests more
authentic

As THE WORLD pulled out of the Depression in the mid-1930s, coverage of cricket on the radio expanded. By 1934, the ABC had found a way of broadcasting Test matches from England. The 'synthetic' commentary, came live from a Sydney studio. Ball by ball, commentators would simulate the game's events based on cables received from England with a sound effects man providing applause and crowd noise in the background.

A generation of boys went to sleep listening to the feats of Bradman. Alan Davidson listened to the 1938 series on a bush radio connected to a car battery. The aerial went up a gum tree and young Alan laid his mattress down next to the radio listening to the first series broadcast live from England by shortwave. When the line dropped out the ABC reverted to synthetic commentary. In Brian Booth's home in Perthville as many as 30 neighbours would cram into the kitchen to listen to matches from England. The Benaud family sat around the family's big Kreisler radio in Jugiong and listened to the Ashes Tests.

Backyard Tests became closer to the real thing. The ABC commentaries seeped deep into the subconscious of the boys of this generation. Players, field settings and the strokes played mirrored what they heard on the radio. They started to write down the results of their backyard Tests in scorebooks. They battled away on a variety of pitches, Benaud on a verandah, Davidson on a home-made turf pitch, Lawry on the street, Simpson on a disused tennis court.

Alan Davidson

PITCH: Home-made dirt pitch.

BAT: Normal bat.

BALL: Cork insides of discarded six stitchers.

WICKET: Three gum tree sticks.

PLAYERS: Mostly by himself, but sometimes with uncle or grandfather.

BACKYARD DRILLS: Stone throwing at posts, catching practice with oranges, batting practice in front of Mum's mirror.

PLAYERS' COMFORT LEVEL: Isolated. As eldest boy on a farm, played mainly by himself.

Just like Charlie Macartney, Alan Davidson's first memory of cricket is batting at his grandfather's orchard in the bush, north of Sydney. While Macartney started as a five year old dispatching excess apples with his home-made bat near Maitland, Davidson first took strike at the age of two on a property at Niagara Park. It was the summer of 1931 and Alan had been given his first bat for Christmas. Facing up to a tennis ball on a concrete path that led to the washing line, he employed a left-handed grip and a right-handed stance. His cricket-mad relatives decided to follow the hands, not the feet. They turned Alan around and a left-handed batsman was born.

The Davidson clan knew what they were doing. His father Keith was one of three boys, all decent club cricketers. Alan's maternal grandfather, Paddy Clifton, was a prolific opening batsman with four cricket playing sons, two of whom played first-grade in Sydney. At one stage, Paddy put together a team of his sons and grandsons. They took on the local Gosford District XI and beat them. When Clifton didn't have a piece of willow in his hand, he was chopping down other types of timber in the Central Coast hinterland. He had a bullock team and his own logging business. At the age of five, Alan and his family moved to a property that adjoined his grandfather's place. Paddy Clifton was to have a huge influence on his grandson's cricket career.

'Even when I was a little bloke,' Davidson recalls, 'My grandfather would say "you've got to learn how to play with a straight bat, son". All I wanted to do was slog.' Young Alan would go along and watch the local Lisarow side play in Black's Paddock and learn off his uncles and grandfather. 'Observation is the best teacher,' Davidson says. 'I learned a lot off them.' When he made his first-grade debut for Lisarow as a 14 year old, his grandfather was still showing the way. Paddy and his son Vern put on 166 for the first wicket in one of Alan's first games in the top grade.

Like his friend and colleague Richie Benaud, Alan spent much of his formative years playing by himself. Being the eldest child in a rural community, he had little choice. While his older relatives were all cricketers, they had jobs to go to during the day. When he was around 12, Alan built his own bush wicket. Using a mattock and shovel he dug a pitch into a hill in a nearby paddock. Using the old cores of the Lisarow team's split and discarded six stitchers, he bowled away at three gum tree sticks placed at one end of the pitch. Accuracy was essential. As Davidson wrote '. . . a mis-directed delivery would bounce crazily down-hill into the scrub, necessitating a tedious search.' Davidson became one of the most accurate bowlers in Test cricket. He was always at the batsman, and conceded less than two runs for every six balls bowled.

The Davidson family orchard helped with Alan's fielding drills. 'I used to get these green oranges, always before Dad came home, and I'd throw them up in the air and run after them and catch them. Of course if I let them hit the ground they'd burst. That's where I learned to catch. Regardless of where I threw them, to me there was no catch that was impossible.' His extraordinary catching feats earned him the nickname 'The Claw'. Don Bradman wrote of Davidson having an '. . . incredible ability to pluck a ball out of the air when to lesser mortals it seemed already past him'.

Even as a boy Davidson's catching ability stood out. As a ten year old he filled in for Lisarow's second-grade team in a final against Narara. Early in the innings he'd already earned his keep by taking a catch at square leg just centimetres off the ground. But with the opposition team needing just five to win with one wicket in hand, the opposition batsman tried to win the match with one shot. He skied the ball to mid-on where Davidson was fielding. Fielders ran from everywhere trying to get under the ball, fearful that a ten year old would muff the chance, but Keith Davidson calmly yelled out, 'Let the kid take it, he won't drop it.' Keith was right to have faith, the catch was taken and Lisarow won the competition.

While young Alan plucked unripe oranges to work on his catching, he used stones to work on his arm. Making his way to and from school along dusty bush tracks, he ran at the rocks scattered along the road, picked them up and pinged them at fence posts. 'When you're running you've got to allow a difference for the angle,' Davidson says, 'It made a hell of a difference to my fielding.' Davidson was able to hit the stumps at will. Johnnie Moyes called him 'one of the master fielders of all history'. Bradman wrote, 'Some of his run outs were phenomenal.' In one of his early first-grade games for Northern Districts he threw out three batsmen in an innings. Davidson attributes his ability to retrieve and throw in one motion to his stone-throwing as a boy.

Practising his batting at Lisarow proved more difficult. While he occasionally got a hit from one of his uncles or his grandfather, normally he had to go it alone. One drill he developed along the bush tracks in his neighborhood helped sharpen his eye. 'If I was walking along the road and saw a gum stick that was an inch and a half thick, I'd pick it up. Then I'd pick up some stones and toss them in the air and try to hit them.'

At home he worked on another batting drill. 'I was given a book called *Cricket Crisis* by Jack Fingleton,' Davidson recalls, 'and on the front of that book is a photograph of Walter Hammond playing a magnificent off-drive with Bertie Oldfield behind. It just looked so absolutely majestic. Mum had a big wardrobe with a mirror in it and I used to get this book and put it on a chair out in front of me and I used to stand in front of that mirror and practise and try and get in the same position as where Walter Hammond was.'

It's no surprise the off-drive became his best shot. When Australia was in dire trouble in 1961 at Manchester with a lead of 157 with just one wicket in hand, it was Davidson's off-drive that helped them retain the Ashes. English off-spinner David Allen had taken three quick wickets on a final day pitch that was turning. Davidson went after England's danger man, clearing the fence twice and taking 20 off an over. Allen was taken off and replaced by an inferior spinner. Davidson and McKenzie put on 98 for the last wicket. Benaud bowled his team to an improbable victory, Australia winning by just 54 runs.

But it was Davidson's new ball bowling that more often won Test matches for Australia. Coming left arm over the wicket and moving the ball both ways, he was able to punch holes in the strongest of batting line-ups. In a Test career that spanned 44 Test matches, he took 186 wickets at the exceptional average of 20.53. But up until the age of 17, Davidson never got his hands on the new ball. At 16 he bowled left-arm leg-breaks. At barely 160 centimetres, he was not the ideal height to bowl quick. But within a year he grew another 18 centimetres. The day before Lisarow took on Wyong in a local competition final, Vern Clifton asked his nephew to give him some practice. Vern had bought a new ball and wanted to face some fast stuff. When young Davo let rip the first ball with a fast inswinger he clean bowled his uncle. The next day he took the new ball and repeated the dose hitting the stumps of Wyong's best bat Micky Baker first ball. His days as a spinner were numbered. Within a couple of years he was representing Australia as an opening bowler.

The bush lifestyle provided the ideal grounding for someone taking on the tiring task of bowling quick on unforgiving pitches. Alan put muscle on his frame by digging fence posts, chopping wood and doing other farm work. In school holidays he went timber cutting with his grandfather. While Charlie Macartney built up his strength as a teenager loading wool bales on the Sydney wharves, Davidson spent his weekends lugging hessian bags full of wheat and chaff. One of his uncles drove a truck and did deliveries for the local store. Alan carried 230 pound bags on his back between the store, the truck and the homes they delivered to. 'I think back to those days and think what a tremendous asset they were to building up my strength,' Davidson recalls.

Davidson would need to be strong and durable. Many times in the Test arena he had to battle through injury and exhaustion. The day before the Lord's Test of 1961 his back was so bad he couldn't stand up straight. With Benaud out with a shoulder injury and Harvey filling in as captain Davidson had to play. Without the benefits of modern-day physiotherapy to fall back on, he had some liniment rubbed into his back and was sent out to bowl. He took 5/42 from 24 overs on the first day, which set up victory in the famous Battle of the Ridge Test. On the 1959 tour of India, he bowled a whole day unchanged in 38 degree heat at Kanpur. In one of Test cricket's most extreme acts of endurance, Davidson sent down 57.3 overs (out of a total of 144) and took 7/93.

Alan Davidson, as he puts it, was 'born to cricket'. His family on both sides was obsessed with the game, and he was brought up in the perfect environment to foster his considerable abilities. 'The biggest thing I had was the freedom of open spaces,' Davidson recalls. 'There was nothing to stop me doing the things I wanted to do.'

Cricket is still popular in the area, but Lisarow no longer has as much open space. There are still some semi-rural properties in the neighborhood, but McMansions are more commonplace. Black's Paddock is now a Sara Lee factory. The orchards on the Davidson and Clifton properties are gone, and with it the old home-made pitch. Backyard cricket is still played out the back of the Davidsons' old house in Awaba Street, the current owners have a cricket-obsessed son, but what's left of the property awaits further subdivision.

Richie Benaud

PITCH: Storeroom floor and back verandah.

BAT: First bat a small one made from packing-case timber.

BALL: Tennis ball.

WICKET: None used at Jugiong or North Parramatta. Had to guess as to whether he was out bowled or not.

RULES: Test match rules, imaginary field set, if in the air to a fielder, out. If hit through the gap, runs. Batted through Test team 1–11.

HAZARDS: None, but there was a shortage of space in the storeroom and the back verandah.

PLAYERS: Richie by himself at home, with neighbours in the local paddock and park.

BACKYARD DRILLS: Hitting ball against the wall, bowling at marks on the ground.

PLAYERS' COMFORT LEVEL: Isolated. But loving it.

In his later years as a commentator, Richie Benaud had an audience in the millions. But at the beginning of his cricketing life, in the isolated country town of Jugiong, he had only himself to entertain. Richie first put bat on ball as a five-year-old, playing alone within the four walls of a disused Department of Education storeroom. His father Lou was the sole teacher at Jugiong Public School between 1932 and 1937. The school, around 350 kilometres south-west of Sydney, had 23 students of various ages, some of whom travelled to school on horseback. After school hours, there were no kids around to share Richie's developing passion for cricket. His father came to the rescue, giving him a home-made bat and a tennis ball, and clearing out an old storeroom attached to the school.

As a Test cricketer Richie Benaud played aggressively. He scored his runs fast, bowled probing leg-spin and was renowned as an attacking captain. But there, on his own, with his little cut-down bat made from packing-case timber, young Richie started off by playing two shots, the forward defence and the back foot defence. For most kids, slogging across the line is all they want to do when they first pick up a bat. So what was a young boy on the banks of the Murrumbidgee doing blocking a tennis ball against a wall? It sounds more like the formative years of Geoffrey Boycott or Trevor Bailey, not a man who would go on to score one of Test cricket's fastest centuries.

Lou Benaud knew exactly what he was doing. If Richie was to learn how to bat, he had to start with the basics. Lou was a top-class cricketer who'd been denied the opportunity to push for state selection. In 1925, the Department of Education shipped him off to One Tree Farm Provisional School, around 1000 kilometres north of Sydney. He spent the next 12 years teaching at various country schools. At least three times he had to turn down the chance to trial before state selectors. The same Department of Education that sent Bill O'Reilly to the backblocks in his prime didn't allow Lou Benaud the opportunity to further his cricket in Sydney. The latter part of his country stint coincided with the Great Depression, so Lou didn't have much choice; he had to hold on to his job and accept his lot.

In that storeroom at Jugiong, young Richie learned more than just defensive shots. Soon he progressed to playing Test matches against the wall. Like Bradman against the tank stand in Bowral, he picked an English XI and an Australian XI, set an imaginary field and threw the ball against the wall, hitting it off the rebound. Just like Bowral, the pitch was undercover, maximising game time during wet weather. The enclosed walls meant he didn't have to spend valuable time chasing balls. Whereas Bradman used a golf ball and a stump, Benaud used a tennis ball and cut-off bat. For a boy of five or six it was perfect training. As Benaud wrote in *On Reflection*, 'Coming from only 15 feet and bouncing, it could be a reasonably difficult assignment. It certainly improved my eye!'

Richie played for hours in the storeroom. Although he'd never seen a Test match, he imagined he was playing for Australia, racking up runs against England like his hero Bradman. The thud of the tennis ball hitting repetitively against the walls filtered back into the school residence. 'It was sweet music to hear the ball being hit in that room,' Lou Benaud remembered, 'For it signified that Rich had developed a keenness for cricket.'

When Richie was seven, the Benaud family moved back to Sydney. Lou had scored a job at Burnside Public School, North Parramatta. The family took up residence a kilometre from the school at 5 Sutherland Road. Richie's younger brother, John, who also played Test cricket, was not born until Richie was 13, so he continued to play his one-man Tests, this time against a brick wall on the back verandah. He chose cricketers from a book his father had given to him – the 1938 *NSW Cricket Association Yearbook* that included all the scorecards from the 1936/7 Ashes series. He placed his imaginary field, and worked hard at piercing the gaps.

Rene Benaud kept a beautiful garden, but that didn't mean her son had to modify his range of strokes. 'My mother grew to understand that the really important thing was that I'd made 29 playing against England this day, and if there was a pot plant or two that had to be renovated that was OK,' Benaud recalls. There was one plant in the back garden that young Richie wouldn't have minded demolishing. Australian children of his generation were force-fed chokos at mealtime. This tasteless vegetable grew like prickly pear on backyard fences across the country. Because of its easy availability it became a staple of family diets throughout the 1930s and 1940s. Richie was often issued the ultimatum; 'eat your vegetables or you can't go out to play cricket'.

Richie's verandah Test matches were taken very seriously. He wrote the scores in his *Unrivalled Pocket Cricket Scoring Book*. Once full, he rubbed them out and started again. Unsurprisingly he called these games as if he was part of the ABC Radio commentary team. Richie was part of the first generation who grew up with cricket on the radio. The ABC started their 'synthetic' broadcasts of Test matches from England in 1934. At Jugiong the 1936–37 Ashes series was heard through 2CO Corowa with the deep-voiced Mel Morris on the microphone. The Benaud family's big Kreisler radio was always tuned in. When Bradman took the Australian team to England in 1938, shortwave broadcasts beamed the commentary live from England for the first time. It was the beginning of a ritual that inspired the Test cricketers of future generations; young boys drifting off to sleep listening to their crystal sets, dreaming that they might one day play for Australia against England at Lord's.

In January 1940, Richie saw his first game of first-class cricket. Aged nine, his father took him by bus, steam train and toast-rack tram to the SCG to watch New South Wales play South Australia. Over 30,000 came to what was one of the last Sheffield Shield matches before the war intervened. It was so crowded that Richie sat in the aisle with his dad in the old Sheridan Stand. Leg-spinner Clarrie Grimmett dominated, taking 6/118. This performance had a big influence on Richie. After the game he told his father that he wanted to bowl leg-spin. But Lou Benaud put a temporary halt to that idea. He believed wrist spin put too much strain on the tendons and ligaments of a young boy. Richie wasn't allowed to bowl leg spin until he was 12. Even now he passes on the same advice to inquiring parents.

Richie could not have had a better mentor than his father. He was there for him at every stage, from crafting him a bat at Jugiong to coaching him in the intricacies of leg-spin in his teen years. Lou instilled in Richie that there was a right way to play cricket. 'Cricket was talked breakfast, lunch and dinner in the Benaud household, every day I can remember,' Richie recalls. 'It was drilled into me over meal tables at home when I was a child that cricketers who do not set about trying to win the game from the start of the match would never be successful, but don't forget the game must be played in the right spirit.' It was this attitude that Benaud carried through into his captaincy of the Australian side. In the 1960s, he helped revive international cricket with positive, aggressive play, at a time when Test matches had become bogged down in negative tactics and meaningless draws.

Lou Benaud also encouraged his son to practise and play the game whenever he could. When Richie wasn't playing his verandah Test matches he would join boys in the neighbourhood for a game in the paddock across the road. The boys built a dirt pitch by digging out the grass and levelling it with a shovel. They watered the pitch and occasionally flattened it out with a roller borrowed from a nearby tennis court. When the boys wanted a truer surface they headed up to Belmore Park (now named Richie Benaud Oval) where a concrete pitch had been laid. Children growing up in suburban Sydney at the time were blessed with plenty of open fields in which to play informal games of sport.

When Richie turned 12 he was able to turn his mind to leg-spin. Two years after watching Grimmett knock over New South Wales, he continued to be inspired by the Fox. He started a backyard bowling drill like Grimmett's but without the fox terrier. 'Bowling at a white mark made on the grass came from an article I had read, written by Grimmett,' Benaud recalls. '[He] said that from the moment he turned to start his run his eyes were fixed on the spot where he wanted the ball to land. I continued to do the same for the rest of my cricket career because it seemed a perfectly logical thing to do. Why would you look anywhere else? Even on the back verandah at Sutherland Road, when bowling the tennis ball against the brickwork, I would look at the spot on the wall I wanted the ball to hit.' Benaud continued this form of practice into his Test playing years. When he had no one else to bowl to in the nets he placed a handkerchief down on a good length, and worked away at improving his accuracy.

Soon after the Benauds came back to Sydney, Lou was drafted back into Cumberland's first-grade side. This introduced Richie to the world of men's cricket at a young age. 'I was able to go to the Tuesday and the Thursday practices and I was allowed to field and it taught me not to fear the cricket ball, it came pretty fast.' The lack of fear was to become an important ingredient in Richie's makeup as a cricketer. He was a courageous hooker of fast bowling and nerveless close-in fielder. At 19, he lost a year of cricket after he shattered the frontal bone in his forehead while trying to hook Victorian quick Jack Daniel. His wedding day toast was sipped through a straw after a taking a ball in the mouth while fielding in the gully in a Test match. But Richie didn't become timid. He hooked Tyson, Hall, Trueman and other quicks with courage and skill throughout his career. Playing for a Combined XI against South Africa on a bouncy Perth deck, Barry Shepherd asked him to take on Peter Pollock, whose pace was troubling team mates. Benaud belted 132.

As a youngster Richie would do anything to be around cricket. At the age of 12, he became the designated scorer for the Cumberland second-grade side. Each Saturday he would pack his whites in case someone failed to show up. That season he was called on twice. In his second-grade debut he had to go in to bat at number 11 with four runs needed for victory. He saw out the over, and his partner belted the next ball over the boundary to win the game. Not many players can say they played second-grade while still in their first year at high school. At 15, Richie played his first full season in grade. At 16, he made his debut in first-grade with his father by his side. In his second game in firsts he scored 98. It probably came as no surprise to Lou. Richie had made a habit of successfully taking on older opponents. His first game of cricket was for Jugiong against Bookham Public. At just six years of age he scored 12 runs against boys nearly twice his age facing a compo ball on a bouncy coir mat pitch.

Lou Benaud had a huge impact on Richie's career. He knew what it took to make it in cricket. He wrote in *The Young Cricketer* 'If you want to reach the top of the cricket ladder you must literally eat, drink and sleep cricket. Half measures will not get you to the top. Outside school hours or working hours you must spend your time at the game – playing it, practising it, conditioning yourself for it, reading about it and looking at first-class matches. When you become such a fanatic you only need the opportunities to get you to the top.' It was this kind of fanaticism that Richie was brought up on and that helped him make it to the top. Like Martin Chappell, who'd been denied opportunities to play first-class cricket during the war years, Lou Benaud was determined to give his sons every opportunity to make it in cricket. Richie was fortunate to be born with talent and parents who helped him cultivate it.

So what of a boy growing up in the same environment today? In 2008 Jugiong Public School celebrated its 125th anniversary and had 15 students. A child living there now wouldn't have to play in a disused storeroom. The school has some flash new cricket nets, funded in part by donations of memorabilia from its most famous ex-pupil. The old Benaud backyard at North Parramatta is still there in all its sprawling glory. While the old verandah is now enclosed, you could easily practise your leg-spinners down the back. It would, however, be hard to get a game happening at the old paddock across the road from 5 Sutherland Road. There's not much activity there anymore, it's currently used as an aged-care facility.

Bob Simpson

PITCH: Disused clay tennis court in Illawarra Road, Marrickville.

BAT: Normal cricket bat

BALL: Six stitchers and other balls salvaged from the Cooks River.

WICKET: A piece of concrete from a nearby quarry.

PLAYERS: Bob and brothers Bill and Jack.

RULES: No runs scored. All about survival.

BACKYARD DRILLS: Fielding drill with a wet tennis ball, mini-cricket games played on concrete in the backyard.

PLAYERS' COMFORT LEVEL: Tough and competitive. Playing against two older brothers who went on to play first-grade.

Street cricket would've proved difficult for the Simpson boys of 517 Illawarra Road, Marrickville, back in the 1940s. A tram line cut through the middle of their bustling street in Sydney's inner west. The unpaved gutters provided plenty of loose rocks for working on your throwing technique, but pulling out the bat and ball might have been fatal. Fortunately, Marrickville in those days had plenty of wide open spaces – market gardens, paddocks and parks, even an old tip. Even better, 50 yards left of the Simpson family's front gate were some disused tennis courts. These courts became the perfect battleground for Bill, Jack and young Bobby to hone their skills as cricketers.

The court was made of clay. The boys watered it and worked on it with an old roller they found in the neighbourhood. For the stumps they dragged a piece of concrete from a nearby quarry. Finding an endless supply of cricket balls was not a problem either. Countless fields adjoined the nearby Cooks River. Any balls hit into the river would end up caught in the reeds. It was the youngest brother's job to source this endless supply of free balls, some of them only a few overs old. And the pitch? 'It played pretty well,' Bob remembers, 'it spun a bit, but it was pretty true.'

It must've spun a bit. All three Simpson boys bowled leg-spin and all three went on to play first-grade: Bill with Wests and Marrickville; Jack with Sydney University and Petersham-Marrickville; Bob with Petersham-Marrickville and Wests. An impressive feat when you consider that unlike Richie Benaud they didn't have a father who could teach them cricket's most difficult art form. Their father Jock was a fine footballer – he emigrated from Scotland in the 1920s where he played professionally for Stenhousemuir FC. But he wasn't a cricketer.

From the age of seven, Bob learned to compete with bigger, stronger older opponents, something that proved useful when he debuted for New South Wales aged just 16. Bill was seven years older, Jack three years older. 'It was a tough school,' Simpson recalls. It was a toughness Bob seemed willing to reciprocate. When he bowled at his brother Jack in an under 21s Poidevin-Gray game he appealed for LBW even though he knew his brother had hit the ball. Jack was not happy. 'He didn't let me forget for months how I had cheated him – he reckoned it was a poor thing for a little brother to do!'

Bob Simpson didn't just learn mental toughness on that old clay court; he also learned discipline and shot selection. 'On one side you had the tennis courts being used, on the other side it was all blackberry bush, so we quickly learnt not to hit the ball in the air over the fence. I just wonder whether that had something to do with the fact I never really wanted to hit the ball in the air.' It's no surprise Simpson got a taste for the big innings either. At Tempe Technical High schoolyard games of cricket were continuous. You batted until someone got you out. Young Bobby was known to bat for days. 'I suppose that's where you get the determination from,' he laughs. Some Tempe old boys might have some understanding for how England felt at Old Trafford in 1964 when Simpson made 311 in nearly 13 hours, across three days.

Bob Simpson is still regarded as one of the best slips fieldsmen in the history of Test cricket. He took 110 catches in 62 Tests, the best ratio of anyone with over 70 catches. New South Wales skipper Keith Miller first placed him there as a 17-year-old in 1953/4. Simpson ran on the field as a substitute fieldsman and asked his skipper where he wanted him to field. 'Oh, I don't know laddie, there is a hole over there. That will do you,' said Miller as he pointed at first slip. Within an hour he'd taken two catches. Next season he took 15 chances out of 16 and he had a job for life. Bob puts his sure hands down to techniques he learned catching wet tennis balls at the beach on family holidays as a nine or ten-year-old. 'I wasn't aware of this at the time, of course, nor could I have known that catching wet tennis balls is ideal training. Unless you have soft hands and perfect coordination the ball won't stick.'

The Simpson boys pegged balls at each other for hours, bouncing them off the wet sand or the water, or using a tree branch to edge catches. 'I think it was then I learnt to let the ball come to me and to turn side on to the ball and not grab at it and develop this sort of softness of movement. I'm sure that's where it came from.' He wasn't to know it at the time but the wet tennis ball was teaching Simpson a technique that would be passed down through generations of Australian cricketers. 'I developed methods which suited me down in the sand that were exactly the same as what I performed in Test matches. There's quite a few people, like Mark Taylor and Ian Chappell, they probably wouldn't like to admit it, but when you look at their stance they were absolute clones of what I was doing.'

Simpson wasn't the first to recognise the benefits of practising catching with tennis balls. Don Tallon, regarded by many as Australia's greatest ever gloveman, practised on dew-soaked tennis balls in his backyard at Bundaberg. Hugh Trumble, who captained Australian in 1901/2 and was recently inducted to the Australian Cricket Hall of Fame, practised his slip fielding by throwing a tennis ball against a brick wall. New Zealand cricketer Daniel Reese wrote about Trumble's practice methods in *Was it All Cricket?* '… his theory being that it is impossible to retain hold of an air [tennis] ball if one snatches at it. This practice accounts for the easy manner in which he always allowed the ball to fall into his hand, for it is also fatal to snatch at a cricket ball.'

When Simpson became Australian coach in 1986, he not only passed on the catching skills he'd learned on the beach at Blue Bay, but he also used fielding drills based on games he and his mates improvised at Petersham-Marrickville. While waiting to bat or bowl in the nets they would set up drills where you had to defend part of the oval like a portion of the fence, or the goalposts. A batsman nicked balls with a bat or a stump and the fielders behind had to defend their patch of turf.

As a boy growing up in Sydney's inner west in the 1940s, Simpson was extremely fit. No lifts from Mum or PlayStation to contribute to adolescent muscle waste. As soon as Bob got home from school he threw the schoolbooks in the corner of his room and headed outside to play cricket or golf, not returning till dinnertime. On Sunday mornings he caddied at Bonnie Doon golf course, often running the 4 kilometres to the course before lugging another player's clubs round for 18 holes and heading home. As he got older his winter sports routine consisted of golf on a Saturday morning, soccer on a Saturday afternoon, tennis Sunday morning and baseball Sunday afternoon. On Saturday night he went dancing to help improve his footwork. Simpson was cross training before the term was invented. Often he walked to games to save the train fare. 'I think all of those things lead to well-rounded kids not just physical fitness, but rhythm, flexibility and good movement,' Simpson says.

If a family of boys was growing up in the old Simpson home of 517 Illawarra Road today, 'rhythm, flexibility and movement' might not be all that's missing. That old disused tennis court has disappeared as well. It seems property speculation now outranks cricket when it comes to games of choice in Sydney's inner west. The old site on Illawarra Road has been cleared in preparation to build over 100 units. Just down the road a group of kids could still organise a hit on the astroturf wicket at Steel Park, but the unique environment that acted as a nursery for Simpson's talents is gone forever. A young cricketer in the making could go to the nearby PCYC on Illawarra Road and play indoor soccer, learn Latin dance or do Pilates, but it's hard to imagine it would develop the kind of hard-nosed cricketer that Bob Simpson became.

Suburban Sprawl –
The post-war building
boom creates a nation
of cricket pitches

AUSTRALIAN CITIES UNDERWENT a massive building boom after the war. Land in fringe suburbs was subdivided into quarter-acre blocks and sold off to young families. Modest sized homes were built, leaving plenty of room down the back for a cricket pitch. It was these big backyards that proved the perfect training grounds for a cohort of combative cricketers.

The five most dominant cricketers in Australia's world champion team of the 1970s grew up in big suburban backyards. The Chappell brothers played their Tests on a big block in Graymore in suburban Adelaide. Dennis Lillee had a series of yards to choose from in Belmont near Perth airport. Rod Marsh's backyard in Armadale, south of Perth, backed onto a vacant block. In Sydney, Jeff Thomson bowled bouncers at his four brothers in their Bankstown backyard.

While other cricketers of the era like Doug Walters and Rick McCosker had the open spaces of rural Australia to learn their craft in, this was an era dominated by suburban boys. They were tough cricketers raised on uncompromising backyard Test matches played against unforgiving brothers and mates.

The Chappell Brothers

PITCH: Home-made turf pitch.

BAT: Normal bats.

BALL: Proper cricket balls.

WICKET: Wooden stumps.

PLAYERS: Ian, Greg, Trevor, Champ the dog and sometimes neighbourhood kids.

RULES: Automatic wicketkeeper and slips. LBWs accepted. If you hit the wire cages on the full you were out. Hitting the leg-side fence between the beams on the full was out. Broken windows were automatically out.

HAZARDS: Hard ball with no protective equipment. A hump in the pitch meant steep bounce. Ian's ruthless streak, Greg's pitch-watering and Trevor's tomahawk.

BACKYARD DRILLS: Fielding practice against the tank stand, batting practice against the laundry wall.

PLAYERS' COMFORT LEVEL: Extreme pressure. Volcanic tempers. Hard balls. High standard of skill. Possibly the most brutal backyard cricket environment known to mankind. But they loved it.

When Greg Chappell was quizzed about his Test debut, an initiation that saw him face the pace of John Snow on a bouncy Perth pitch, it was put to him that starting out in Test cricket must've been a tough experience. 'No mate, not at all,' Greg said to his inquisitor, 'the toughest cricket I played was in the backyard against my older brother. After playing in the backyard against Ian, Test cricket was a breeze.'

Maybe Greg wasn't overstating it. On his Test debut he made a hundred. In one of his earlier games in the backyard with Ian he was cracked on his gloveless fingers and given an earful. 'Normally, Ian stood about 10 metres away and glared at me until I got up,' Greg wrote, 'but on this occasion he'd come right up the pitch. I thought, "at last, a bit of compassion from the older brother". So I looked up, tears in my eyes, and he said, "I wouldn't worry about the fingers if I was you, it's your head next".' Ian was four years older than Greg. A ball at the head must've been a terrifying prospect.

Their backyard battleground was situated at 4 Leak Avenue, Graymore, an Adelaide suburb popular with young families after World War II. The streets of Graymore were named after Victoria Cross winners. Valour was certainly required in the backyard of the Chappell home. All three boys played with a proper cricket ball from the age of two. Their father Martin wanted to make sure they played without fear. 'I'm sure there was a bit of method in the madness,' says Greg. 'Dad insisted we play with a hard ball all the time so we got to understand what it was like, but he didn't give us any pads or gloves to play with. I think the method behind that was you better learn that the bat is your best defence, and if you use that properly you won't need much protection elsewhere.'

The hard ball was even tolerated inside the family home.

'Martin would be walking around the house,' recalls Ian, 'and suddenly he'd just go bang and he'd throw a ball at you without giving you any warning.' Martin's indoor slips training routines obviously worked. Ian snared 105 Test catches; Greg held the world record upon retirement with 122. However, insisting his children play with a hard ball did come at a cost. When asked what went into creating three Test cricketers, Martin said, 'All my spare cash, all my leisure time and about 150 broken windows.'

Martin Chappell played district cricket in Adelaide for 22 years. One season he topped the district averages, and for a brief period was in the state squad. While he represented South Australia in baseball, he never played Sheffield Shield cricket. His best years, like many men of that era, were lost to World War Two. But he was determined to turn his three sons into Test cricketers. On his wife's side, the family had already produced one Test cricketer. Jeanne Chappell was the daughter of Victor Richardson, former captain of Australia, and regarded as the best all-round sportsman to emerge from South Australia.

The Chappell home was the ideal place to cultivate the talents of the three cricket-mad boys. The backyard was 24 metres wide, which allowed room for a full-length pitch and a three pace run-up. A turf pitch was constructed from Athelstone soil, a clay soil used on the Adelaide Oval pitches. The side fence served as the automatic wicketkeeper and the slips. The house was situated on the off side, and the glass louvres on the back porch challenged the wisdom of Martin's decision about playing with a hard ball. But he solved this by acquiring some wire mesh gates from the local tip, and placing them in a row in front of the glass. The leg side was full of fruit trees which were protected by wire cages that doubled as fielders. Martin extended the height of the side fences to protect the neighbours' windows. 'In the end,' Greg wrote in *Cricket: The Making of Champions*, 'our backyard was like Stalag 17.'

Greg's unique flick-off-the-hip shot, which gave him many runs in Test cricket, came about because of those fielding cages in front of the fruit trees. 'There was a gap,' Greg wrote, 'between forward square leg and backward square leg, between the citrus and almonds, so the only place I could really hit the ball on the leg side with safety was just behind square. That's how I learnt to pick the ball up off my hip.' Coaches and opponents found the shot difficult to comprehend. Mike Brearley, who captained England against Greg's Australian sides in 1977 and 1979/80, wrote of it in an envious manner, 'There's no name for this shot. Very few batsmen can play it … most people are just nudging it around the corner, but he plays it with a free flow of the bat.' If he'd seen the Chappells' backyard he might've understood where it came from.

The backyard games of cricket at Leak Avenue were played like authentic Test matches. Ian was Australia and Greg was England. When Ian grew out of these games, Greg became Australia and Trevor had to play for the Poms. Greg, who ended up with the best Test record of the three, got the best of both worlds. He learned how to struggle and survive against Ian, and how to dominate and be ruthless against Trevor.

Each brother batted down the scorecard, according to the Test line-ups of the day. If a left-hander, like Neil Harvey was due in, they batted left-handed. When you were out, you had to leave the crease, put your bat under your arm and walk over to the tank stand. There you wrote your score and mode of dismissal into the scorebook. The figures couldn't be fudged, but you could swap the players around. 'Keith Miller was my favourite player,' recalls Ian, 'and I know if Miller got out for a low score I'd rub his name out and put someone else's name there. As soon as I made a hundred or a decent score that would be Keith Miller, so Keith Miller never failed.' The laundry doubled as the pavilion, and after your dismissal you had to come back out through the laundry door as the next batsman.

All three brothers played for keeps. Ian used a ridge on the pitch to extract extra bounce to try and shift Greg. When Greg took on Trevor he showed no mercy. In one innings Greg scored over 1000 against his little brother. When it was Trevor's turn to bat the conditions often deteriorated. Greg was known for watering the wicket while his younger brother got ready to bat. Trevor was no shrinking violet himself. One time after he was dismissed and sent packing to the laundry, he reappeared with a tomahawk and chased Greg around the backyard. Greg, whose survival skills were just as refined beyond the batting crease, vaulted the gate and ran three blocks down the road before he dared turn around and check on his assailant.

These backyard Test matches were critical to each brother's development. They learned how to survive against a fast moving ball, and respond in game-like situations. They learned how to win, how to lose, how to take wickets and how to score runs. They dealt with pressure and taught themselves how to overcome adversity. They also faced a hell of a lot of balls. Martin Chappell reckoned the backyard pitch was used 300 days a year. 'I spent 22 years in club cricket,' he said, 'but I would say that by the time each one of the boys was 14 he had faced more deliveries than I had in my whole career.'

Beyond the backyard, the boys learned to adapt to different kinds of conditions. At home the backyard pitch played fast but true. But down at the beach they played with a tennis ball that had the fur shaved off one side. In this form of cricket you had to react to balls that moved in the air and skimmed off the water and wet sand. The local park had yet another set of conditions. Here they could get a game against boys of various ages on a deck that was a seamer's paradise. If they wanted a hit of baseball, across the road were some sand hills, perfect for sliding, and for setting up a baseball diamond.

There was another backyard pitch that was critical to the Chappell brothers' development, and that was at the home of Lynn Fuller. Lynn had been a good country cricketer, and after moving to Adelaide, set up a Sunday morning coaching session at his home in North Glenelg. From the age of five each of the Chappell boys started getting lessons from Fuller. Each Sunday, he worked away on their techniques, making sure they could play the forward and backfoot defensive strokes and that they got everything in the right position – the left elbow up, the left knee bent and the head over the ball.

'Lynn taught us the fundamentals,' Greg says, 'and Dad taught us how to bat.' Batting for Martin Chappell meant being able to score runs. After Lynn had finished with the boys, Martin would throw balls at them. He threw wide balls, half volleys, long hops and bouncers. He wanted to make sure they all knew how to make the most of their time spent at the crease and, in particular, be able to put away the bad ball.

Martin Chappell was adamant that his boys would learn early how to play the short ball. Ian remembers at the age of nine Martin telling him to get back in the nets after one of Lynn Fuller's sessions. Martin, using his baseballer's arm, started throwing balls at pace at a ridge halfway along Fuller's pitch. The balls reared up at the head and body of his eldest son. 'I wasn't told to duck or anything,' Ian recalls. 'I always just hooked or pulled and that's where I learnt where to hook and pull.'

In all his years of hooking the best fast bowlers in the world, including Wes Hall, John Snow, Dennis Lillee, Jeff Thomson, Andy Roberts and Michael Holding, Ian Chappell was never hit in the head. 'I got hit over the right eye once when I was 15,' says Ian, 'and I never, ever got hit before that, or after that. And I can thank Martin for that.' All three Chappell brothers had to face the might of the West Indies on sub-standard decks during World Series Cricket. Their formative years in the backyard put them in a better position than most to survive the bombardment from Roberts, Holding, Croft and Garner.

Ian and Greg Chappell both had their ability and mettle tested against men from a young age. 'At 14, I was playing senior cricket,' says Greg, 'at 16, I was playing A grade baseball against tough hardened blokes, some of whom had been off to the war. So it was a tough environment and you learnt to handle yourself and there was no whingeing.' In one of Greg's earliest games in men's cricket, one of Martin's old adversaries from West Torrens fielded in close and sledged Greg about his father, his brother and anything else that popped into his head. It only made him concentrate more. Greg thought, 'Well, bugger you. The more you talk, the longer I'll stay here.'

All three Chappell brothers went to school at Prince Alfred College. When Greg and Ian went through school, the first XI played B Grade in the men's district competition on Saturdays. That meant both Ian and Greg had to test themselves against men from the age of 14. This was crucial for their development. Sometimes they had to face bowlers who had played, or would soon play, first-class cricket. By the time Trevor went through Prince Alfred College things had changed. The first XI played only against other schools. Trevor racked up big scores against other schoolboys, but failed to get the exposure to tough district cricket in his early teens. Both Ian and Greg feel this held back his development. 'I believe,' Ian wrote, 'playing against grown men at a young age gave Greg and myself a huge advantage over Trevor.'

The withdrawal of the schoolboy teams from the district competition isn't the only aspect of Ian and Greg's cricket education that has disappeared. The backyard games that played such an important role in their development would now be impossible in Leak Avenue. Most of the homes have been redeveloped. Gone are those big backyards that dominated the neighbourhood. The Chappells' old home has been knocked down and replaced by two adjoining houses. 'I think it's one of the great tragedies of modern life,' says Greg, 'as far as sport is concerned, that kids don't have those environments anymore. It's one of those things I see as a coach that a lot of the things we learnt in the backyard and around my father and his friends … the little things that add up to making a player a little bit better than being just a good batsmen or a good bowler, I think have been lost because those natural unstructured environments don't exist anymore.'

Greg believes the loss of these kinds of backyards is already having a big impact on the development of young cricketers in Australia, on the way they play, and the way they think. 'Sometimes we played a full Test series in a day so you'd bat ten times in a day; you'd have ten innings so getting out wasn't such a big deal. You didn't enjoy getting out, but it wasn't such a defining moment that it turns you negative in the way you went about your batting.'

The reduction in the amount of unstructured play is something Greg saw with his own boys Stephen and Jon. 'When I saw my kids growing up and playing cricket they weren't having those kinds of innings. They were batting maybe once in the nets during the week, and then on the weekend, and if they got out it was a pretty big event. And it did affect the way they played the next time they batted. Now the young cricketers are only getting those nets. You don't learn to play cricket in the nets because you don't have the decision-making processes you have in a match, and that's what we had in the backyard. It was making decisions in real time.'

Shot selection

Greg Chappell's signature flick-from-the-hip shot was very much a product of his backyard environment. It's not uncommon that the strokes you play repetitively as a child become your strongest shots as an adult.

• • •

Swashbuckling opener Keith Stackpole grew up in Collingwood. His childhood games were played in a delivery lane outside a factory just off Budd Street. Straight bat shots were unproductive – they would crash into the brick wall of the factory. The main gaps were at point and square leg, so young Stackpole had to learn to cut and pull and hook. These were the shots that dominated his batting for years to come.

• • •

Geoff Marsh scored a lot of his Test runs through point and cover. He played much of his early cricket on a verandah at Wandering, south of Perth. On the leg-side were windows leading to his parents' bedroom. Marsh learned to cut and cover drive for reasons of self-preservation. Kim Hughes was similarly strong through the off-side. In the backyard of his childhood home in Floreat Park, leg-side shots weren't on. You were automatically out if you hit the fence or landed it in the flower bed. Hughes's flamboyant down-on-one-knee square drive has been attributed to the layout of that backyard.

• • •

Both Mark and Steve Waugh were adept at working the ball onto the on side thanks to the Lord's-like slope on their front lawn. They went with the movement off the pitch, flicking the ball between midwicket and square leg. Alan Davidson puts his strong off-driving down to rehearsing the stroke repeatedly in front of his mother's wardrobe mirror. Davidson was mimicking a photograph of Wally Hammond off-driving which appeared on the front of Jack Fingleton's book *Cricket Crisis*.

• • •

The shot you can't play in your childhood games can also become your weakness later in life. When Sid Barnes played in the street at Stanmore, there was a window at mid-off. As Barnes wrote, 'Probably that is why, in my career later, I played the off-drive least of all the strokes.' Ray Lindwall relied more on his off-side play due to the pet magpie that lurked at square leg over the neighbour's back fence at Hurstville.

• • •

A number of fast bowlers can blame their parents and their backyard designs for their batting weaknesses. While Jason Gillespie was a master of the forward defence, he struggled with the cross-bat shots. Cut shots or pull shots in his driveway Tests went into the bushes or the fish pond. Both were out. The Lee brothers never mastered the cut shot thanks to the next-door neighbour's fence. It was only 2 metres from the bat on the off-side. If you hit it on the full you were out. Geoff Lawson was never a great cutter either. Behind point in his backyard was an instant dismissal.

Doug Walters

PITCH: Homemade ant-bed pitch or verandah.

BAT: Normal cricket bat.

BALL: Six stitcher.

WICKET: Kerosene tin.

PLAYERS: Doug and brothers Warren and Terry, sister Colleen, parents Ted and May.

RULES: Conventional cricket rules.

HAZARDS: Ant bites on the pitch.

BACKYARD DRILLS: Hitting the ball against the side fence.

PLAYERS' COMFORT LEVEL: Tough Test matches. Played mostly with no pads or gloves, so the hard ball could cause some damage.

The meat ant's contribution to Australian cricket is rarely celebrated. But in the late 1950s on a dairy farm at Raglan, in country New South Wales, the *Iridomyrmex purpureus* played an important role in the development of one of Australia's most entertaining batsmen. For it was there, on a turning pitch made from the dug up meat ant nests, that Doug Walters honed his distinctive batting skills.

Doug Walters was the third of four siblings born into a cricketing family. His father Ted played for the Tillegra B-grade side; his mother May and sister Colleen played in the local women's competition. His brothers Warren and Terry were also keen cricketers. The family lived in or around Dungog for all of Doug's formative years. Wherever the Walters family moved, a cricket pitch was soon built in the backyard.

The Hunter Valley may now be known for its shiraz and semillon, but it's long had a reputation for producing tough and talented sportsmen. Footballers such as Clive Churchill, Andrew Johns and John Sattler, and boxers like the legendary Les Darcy. Johns and Sattler are the sons of coalminers. 'The Little Master' was the son of a Gallipoli veteran. Les Darcy's father Edward was a labourer and like Doug Walters' father, a share-farmer.

Ted Walters worked for years in the timber mills. He took up a lease on a dairy farm at Raglan owned by one of his employers. It was here, using some classic bush ingenuity, that the Walters family built the most sophisticated of their backyard pitches. A suitable site was selected – in front of the outdoor dunny – and the wicket area was dug out. Doug attached a trailer to a tractor, and went bush with his younger  brother Terry. They dug up around twenty meat ant nests and transplanted them to the site of the pitch. Doug used the tractor to plough the ant-bed wicket, before watering it and rolling it. The pitch took a week to build and smooth out.

A kerosene tin was used for a wicket and the fence in front of the old outhouse provided a good backstop to the batsman. The pitch possessed a few hazards foreign to most cricketers. 'It was a little bit hairy,' Doug recalls, 'it made your feet move pretty quickly for the first two or three weeks before the ants really got rolled over.' It's no wonder a few ants sprung to the surface on a good length. A single meat ant nest can contain as many as 64 000 ants. Lucky for the Walters clan, the meat ant's bite is not quite as brutal as a bull ant's. The enduring memory of Bill O'Reilly's first school game was not of the match itself, but of being bitten by a 'jumping joey' while scoring.

Test matches on the ant-bed pitch were often a family affair. Mum, Dad, Colleen and the boys would team up and play three a side. May Walters was particularly hard to dislodge. 'She was pretty stodgy,' laughs Doug. Maybe May was simply too tired to play any shots. She and Ted rose each day at around 3 am to milk the cows. On school mornings the Walters kids left home at 7.30 am and caught the milk truck to school. They arrived in time to get an hour's game in before classes started. On a weekend, or during the holidays, the first session of the ant-bed Tests began around eight, once the last of the milk cans was filled and breakfast was finished.

After school the Test matches resumed. These games went until dark, sometimes beyond. Appealing against the light was frowned upon by the Walters clan. Twenty-odd years before Kerry Packer pioneered night cricket, the Walters family trialled it with Tilly lanterns at Raglan. In those days the farm didn't have any electricity. The kerosene lanterns may have provided just enough light for the morning milking sessions, but they didn't help much when a cricket ball came hurtling at you out of the dark.

These matches took on all the rituals of real Tests. Warren Walters retained the eldest brother's right to play for his country of birth. Doug had to be England or the West Indies. The teams batted from one to eleven. If a batsman like Gary Sobers was due in, Doug had to bat left handed. If Ray Lindwall was bowling Warren had to come in off the long run. A score sheet recorded every ball bowled, every run scored. There were no modified backyard rules or spatial constraints. Like a real Test, these contests could last for days.

The pitch spun sharply. As a general rule, the older the pitch, the more it turns. The ant-bed pitch didn't just have to hold up for five days, it had to last for years. Big cracks appeared after a while and the bowlers homed in on them. Young Doug had to learn to use his feet and get to the pitch of the ball, just as Neil Harvey did on the cobblestone pitch at the back of his house in Fitzroy. This was a skill he would use to great effect in Test cricket. 'It certainly helped me against spin bowlers. I've got no doubt about that,' Doug says, 'because the ant bed did turn quite a lot and you had to use your feet a bit. I've got no doubt at all that was a major contributor to the fact I played spin reasonably well.'

Some of Doug Walters' best innings were against quality spinners on tricky wickets. In 1969/70, facing Bedi, Prasanna and Venkataraghavan on a spinning pitch in Madras, he scored the only century in a game Australia won by 77 runs. 'Deadly' Derek Underwood, a left-arm spinner named in England's greatest post-war XI, relished the battles he had with Walters, describing him as 'a wonderful player of spinners'. At Port of Spain in 1973, Walters dominated on a dusty pitch cooked up to help local hero Lance Gibbs. The West Indies picked three spinners hoping the turning pitch would deliver them a series lead. Gibbs crowded the batsmen with two, sometimes three short legs. Walters's response? He used his feet just as he did on the ant-bed pitch; cracking 102 out of the 138 runs scored between lunch and tea. Ian Chappell regards this as the best innings he's seen on a turning pitch. Once again he was the only batsman to score a century in the match. Australia won by 44 runs.

The ant-bed pitch was not the only deck that got a workout on the Walters property. When rain interrupted their Test matches, they would move to the enclosed verandah, an arena with its own set of rules. 'There was no running between wickets and 2 runs were scored for hitting the side wall past halfway,' Doug wrote in *The Doug Walters Story*, '4 for rolling it into the back wall, and 6 for hitting the back of the verandah on the full.' If you broke a window you were automatically out. At the farm at Raglan they also played games on an open verandah. These were more one-on-one games between Doug and other siblings. If you played a straight drive off the verandah you had to keep it down. The caught and bowled came into play because of the drop-off from the deck to the lawn. 'If you got them a little bit off the ground by the time you hit the end of the verandah they were a couple of feet high coming back to the bowler.'

Having an older brother was good for Doug's cricket. Not only was he getting stiff competition at home, but it dragged him into competitive cricket at an early age. When Warren joined the local under-15 side, Doug went too. He was only ten years old, but soon learned how to deal with a hard ball bouncing off a concrete wicket hurled down by boys five years older. Doug came to learn the value of leg-side shots as well. When he progressed to the local colts team, they played their home matches on a paddock at Dingadee. The outfield had around half a dozen trees on it. The rule was if you hit a part of a tree, it was four, even if you just grazed one of the leaves. At square leg, just 20 metres from the bat, was the closest tree. It became an irresistible target for Doug. 'When I came to Sydney I found I had to change my batting stance because I was too front-on, and I've always blamed that tree!'

While television has been the great teacher for many modern-day cricketers, it was radio that influenced Doug's generation. 'Until I came to Sydney, I had not had much coaching,' he recalled in his autobiography. 'You could almost say I was taught by Alan McGilvray.' McGilvray's ball-by-ball descriptions must've sunk deep into Walters' psyche. In his first Test match he went out to bat facing enormous pressure. The Australian team was 4/125 and Doug was facing bowlers he'd never played against. Fred Titmus was turning his offies and had fielders crowded around the bat. But as Walters told his biographer, Ashley Mallett, in *One of a Kind*, McGilvray's commentaries had prepared him for the big occasion, 'When I finally played against some of these blokes I had never seen, I found myself thinking that I know so much about their approach and mannerisms that I felt like I had been batting against them for a couple of years.' Doug felt so at home he racked up 155 in his first Test innings.

It seems the ABC commentary team was the only set of teachers Walters listened to while growing up. Doug attended Dungog High where he excelled at sport, but not homework. When he told his teachers he didn't need to study hard because he was going to play cricket for Australia, he was told he'd never make it. Walters claims he used this as inspiration to prove his teachers wrong. Those teachers mustn't have been reading the local papers at the time. In one junior match, Walters took the phenomenal figures of 17/11. After progressing to the seniors, he was picked in a combined Maitland side. This was his launching pad into big cricket

Jack Chegwyn was a state selector and former New South Wales batsman. He scored over ten thousand runs in first-grade for Randwick. But Chegwyn's greatest contribution to New South Wales cricket was his talent-spotting abilities. For 30 years he took teams made up of Sydney grade players on tours of the country, looking for players with potential. He recognised that many of the best cricketers came from the bush. Bradman, McCabe and O'Reilly were not only highly skilled, they had a hardiness and self-reliance about them that made them formidable cricketers. Country boys were used to hard work and hard play. Walters fitted this mould. From a young age he'd been working on the farm, and had helped his father clear the land in his timber working days. Like most country boys, he'd been playing sport against men from a young age.

When Jack Chegwyn's XI took on Maitland, Walters was just 16. But he was ready for the big occasion. He scored 51 not out and took four wickets. Chegwyn pencilled Walters into his little book as a player to watch. When another promising cricketer was forced to withdraw from a New South Wales Colts game due to university exams, Walters was called into the team. He scored 140 not out including a famous six that went out of the SCG no.2 ground, across Driver Avenue and into Kippax Lake. Soon he was called into the New South Wales team. There was no mollycoddling of the young Walters. Eight days after his seventeenth birthday he made his debut against Queensland, who at that time had an attack led by West Indian great Wes Hall. After failing in the first dig, Walters batted solidly in the second, scoring 50. He was on his way. Walters moved to Sydney the following year. By the age of 20, he was scoring hundreds for Australia. By the end of his career he'd scored 15 Test centuries, many of them match-winning, crowd-pleasing knocks.

Walters did have his own unique style, on and off the field. His backlift wasn't completely straight, his heels clicked together when he drove. His technique was considered questionable on seaming English pitches. His pre-match relaxation routine involved staying up late and having a few beers. When fitness training became part of professional cricket he wore a 'Jogging Kills' T-shirt in protest. Walters was old school. He didn't practise martial arts, listen to motivational tapes or write cookbooks. Nicotine, alcohol and card games were enough to keep Dougie in peak mental and physical condition. Whatever he did, it worked. In 74 Tests he scored 5357 runs at an average of 48.26. An average comparable to greats like Neil Harvey, Allan Border and Steve Waugh. Ian Chappell always wanted him in his side because he won matches through his fast scoring.

So could a young Doug Walters emerge in the current era? Country New South Wales is still fertile territory for emerging cricketers. Glenn McGrath, Adam Gilchrist, Brett Lee, Phil Jaques and more recently Phillip Hughes have emerged from regional New South Wales. The Hunter Valley still produces tough and talented athletes, but not any of late from dairy farms with ant-bed pitches. It's still true that any cricketer who's good enough can play for Australia, no matter where they come from. But you don't tend to see cricketers as unique as Doug playing first-class cricket these days. Young talented players are placed in development squads and sent to the Centre for Excellence. Batting styles are more uniform. Fitnesss and discipline is paramount. Even having a messy room can get you kicked out of the Cricket Academy. Who knows what they'd do with a larrikin in a 'Jogging Kills' T-shirt?

Dennis Lillee

PITCH: Sandy backyard strip covered with lino at the batsman's end.

BAT: Regular cricket bat.

BALL: Mostly tennis ball, sometimes six stitcher or compo ball.

WICKET: Stumps.

PLAYERS: Dennis, brother Trevor, neighbour Chris, and other boys in the neighbourhood.

RULES: Over the fence was six and out. Hitting the fence on the full was six, the fence on the bounce was four. LBWs allowed (of course).

HAZARDS: Game could be over if the ball was hit into Mr Braithwaite's backyard. Footholds loose due to sandy surface.

PLAYERS' COMFORT LEVEL: Fiercely competitive games. Black sand everywhere.

Watching Dennis Lillee bowl was one of the great joys of cricket in the 1970s and 1980s. With ball in hand, Lillee merged beauty with terror. His run-up and action were classical in their execution. Starting with small rhythmical steps, he built up momentum stride by stride as the crowd chanted his name. At the crease he launched himself towards the batsman with head, arms and torso in perfect position to send the ball down with pace, control and sideways movement. The follow-through rounded it all off with a few last lingering steps placing him within whispering distance of the batsman. But where it all began for Dennis Lillee, in the working-class Perth suburb of Belmont, things weren't quite so smooth.

The young Lillee was a bit of klutz. He fell over easily and had an unusual gait. There was no fast bowler's strut back then. As a boy he had to wear special boots to accommodate a weakness in his ankles. These boots made Dennis heavy on his feet. The boy, whom Fred Trueman would end up describing as 'fast bowling perfection', had to teach himself a different style of walking and running just to stay vertical. He didn't even have a decent fast bowler's run-up. In the early days of the Lillee backyard Tests he bowled off just five paces.

Dennis and his younger brother Trevor played in the backyard, frontyard, or in other parts of the neighbourhood. East Belmont was a housing commission area stacked full of ten pound poms. The houses were fibro, the backyards big and the lawns were patchy. While Western Australia's warm climate and wide open spaces must've tempered any homesickness for the mother country, it's hard to imagine the local lawns eliciting similar feelings. West Australians aren't called Sandgropers for no reason. Perth is a sand-swept city, with particles of grey and black Bassendean sand the dominant strain in Belmont's barren backyards.

The best local pitch lay behind Chris McLeod's home. A couple of palings were removed between the adjoining fence to make access easier. The grassless pitch was covered by a piece of lino at the batsman's end, which helped the ball zip through at a WACA-like pace. The crease at the bowler's end became so worn that an old mattress was dug into it to stop the footholds getting any deeper. The mattress limited the erosion, but proved a wobbly landing point. Taking a short run-up was a matter of necessity, not just because of the footholds, but because there was only room to come in off five steps. But soon Dennis was compelled to lengthen that run-up. He was about to see the great Wes Hall in action.

Wes Hall was one of the most popular cricketers to visit Australia. As a fast bowler he was not unlike Lillee. He had beautiful rhythm, the heart of a lion, and an ability to find himself in the middle of dramatic on-field events. David Frith in *The Fast Men* described the West Indian's style as a 'magnificent bounding approach, eyes bulging, teeth glinting, crucifix flying, climaxing in a classical cartwheel action and intimidating followthrough'. When Frank Worrell's West Indians played Western Australia in 1960/1, Trevor and Dennis jumped the fence and sneaked into the members' area of the WACA. They spied Wes outside the players' pavilion, and approached their hero. 'Wes never tired of answering our questions, most of which were stupid,' Lillee wrote in *Back to the Mark*. 'He seemed to love it and that personal touch made an everlasting impression on me.'

Wes became Lillee's main inspiration. 'All I wanted to do then,' Lillee wrote, 'was to run in a long way and bowl fast.' Those backyard Tests soon had to be relocated to accommodate the long run. There were plenty of options. The Lillee boys grew up in the era of post-war suburban sprawl. They lived in a street full of council homes built on quarter and half-acre blocks. It was the perfect place to play cricket. There were plenty of kids and plenty of public spaces. These games were taken very seriously. When lino wasn't being laid, pitches were mown and rolled. Teams were selected and countries adopted. 'We had all the trimmings,' Lillee recalled, 'umpires, scoreboards and even the odd female spectator.' The scoreboard in Chris McLeod's backyard was fairly straightforward. A piece of chalk was used to mark the scores on the fence. On weekends these Test matches would expand into a full Test series.

Dennis was lucky to have a brother who was only 18 months younger. Trevor had the legendary Lillee competitive streak which meant they were able to push each other to the limits. 'We were very competitive against each other in all our sports, with the usual fights about being out or not,' Lillee wrote. 'I treated him as a younger brother but he was a tough young man and would take no rubbish from anyone, me included.'

When they weren't playing backyard Tests they trained at the local primary school nets. Trevor was an opening batsman, the perfect training partner for a fiery young fast bowler on the make. Trevor played first-grade cricket in Perth at 16, but by the age of 18 he'd found another form of religion, dedicating his weekends to the church. The standard of competition in those backyard games was unrelenting. Dennis rated Trevor a better sportsman than him. Ken Waters, their school cricket coach, rated Chris McLeod (who became a novelist) a better bowler than Dennis.

But even back then Dennis had something over his peers. He was the one prepared to go the extra mile. If he was going to bowl like Wes Hall, he needed to be fit. Hall's run-up at times extended to 40 yards. It helped that Dennis had the right genetic make-up. His father didn't know much about cricket, but he sure had stamina. Keith Lillee was a long-haul truck driver, who'd been a handy amateur footballer in his youth. In shades of Bill

O'Reilly's father's long-distance cycling escapades, Keith used to ride his pushbike around 35 kilometres just to get to football training. But Dennis Lillee's maternal grandfather was to have an even greater influence. Len Halifax was a boxing trainer, described by his grandson as a 'Spartan'. 'He encouraged me to run, run, run and then run some more,' Lillee wrote, 'instilling in me the awareness of the value of being fit enough to last and outlast the toughest of conditions.'

Len Halifax urged Dennis to train so hard he could push through the pain barrier and get his 'second wind'. He ran as often as six nights a week, entering his times in a log book. As Chris McLeod recalls, 'Dennis became very focused on fitness when we started playing at the grade club, Perth – he would go for long training runs, which seemed like bizarre behaviour to me at the time. He was clearly determined to make the most of his (considerable) abilities.' Lillee's fitness levels combined with his will to win made it difficult for batsmen to see him off, even on flat decks. Ian Chappell, who as a captain often got the best from Lillee, regularly asked his spearhead for 'just one more over'. 'He was the most determined cricketer I've ever come across,' Chappell wrote. 'If anyone ever mastered his bowling, which was rare, they still had to overcome his iron will.'

Lillee credits the development of this iron will to Ken Waters, his cricket and football coach at Belmay Primary School. 'He had a big influence on me, developing my will to win and teaching me to never give up,' Lillee recalled. When Western Australia was rolled for 77 in a Gillette Cup match in 1976, Ken Waters was watching on television. 'Come on Dennis,' he said to himself, 'you can do it.' Lillee shouted to his team-mates 'We can win this fucking game!' before charging onto the ground like a man possessed. He bowled Viv Richards for a duck in the first over and had Greg Chappell caught behind soon after. Queensland was skittled for 62.

Waters, an old-fashioned educationalist, believes Dennis Lillee's early years were critical to his success. 'Sporting academies may be producing top sportspeople but I believe those with real grit like Ian Chappell and Dennis Lillee were the product of the schoolyard and their ilk may not be seen again.' Maybe Waters is right. At Lillee's old primary school they don't even have a school cricket team anymore, a story repeated at other schools in the region. A former principal with 47 years' experience in education, Waters has been visiting a range of schools since his retirement, supervising student teachers. He says the introduction of the teaching model known as Outcomes Based Education has killed off school sport. 'Teachers are so bogged down by paperwork that they don't have time to coach cricket teams anymore.'

Cricket in the home playgrounds of Belmont is drying up too. While there are still plenty of parks in the area, many of the housing commission homes, like the Lillees' old place, have been demolished, sold off and subdivided. Those big backyards have been carved up to satisfy the demands of Perth's property market. The cricketers who dominated Australia's world champion team in the mid 1970s were suburban boys. Lillee, Marsh, Thomson and the Chappell brothers were all reared in Darwinian backyard battlegrounds. Time will tell whether the erosion of these competitive environments will create cricketers short on the kind of mongrel needed to win Test matches.

Allan Border

PITCH: Concrete slab in backyard.

BAT: Cricket bat and cricket stump.

BALL: Cricket balls, tennis balls, golf balls, plastic practice golf balls, grapefruits.

WICKET: Rubbish bin.

PLAYERS: Allan and brothers Johnno and Brett.

RULES: Six and out, hit the clothesline or laundry on the full and you're out, automatic wicketkeeper, and one hand, one bounce catches off certain structures.

HAZARDS: Nearby block of flats full of windows and the Mosman Tornado of 1969.

BACKYARD DRILLS: Ball in stocking.

PLAYERS' COMFORT LEVEL: Extreme pressure. Intensely competitive environment.

The backyard cricket games, played at 27 The Crescent, Mosman, in the 1960s were a glazier's delight. The Border family's Sydney home backed onto a block of flats, providing a virtual shooting gallery of windows for Allan and his younger brothers, Johnno and Brett, to strike at. Playing with a six stitcher, the boys smashed the neighbours' windows with such regularity that their father, John, ended up paying all their insurance premiums. The closest window belonged to an elderly neighbour, Miss Cheeseman. But she bore the brunt of the boys' cross-bat shots with astounding tolerance. 'Oh Mrs Border,' she used to say, 'I do so love to hear the boys enjoying themselves.'

An understanding neighbour wasn't all the Border boys had to be thankful for. Despite the windows, the backyard was an ideal arena for a game of cricket. A concrete slab near the laundry made for a good batting deck. The back wall acted as automatic wicketkeeper and first slip. The yard was around 20 metres long, and 15 metres wide, enough room for three boisterous boys to play a competitive match. You had to fight hard to defend your wicket. In these Test matches there were plenty of ways you could get out. Hit the laundry or the clothesline on the full and you were gone. The one hand, one bounce rule was invoked for any shot caught off a vertical structure. Over the fence was six and out and go fetch.

Retrieving the ball after smashing a window could be an awkward experience. But Allan got more than he bargained for after one lofted sweep shot entered a unit. 'As I climbed the fence and peered through the shattered window,' he wrote in *Allan Border: An Autobiography*, 'there she was – my very first naked girl. She'd apparently been sleeping and my sweep shot had rudely disturbed her rest.' The boys didn't need any incentives to smash more windows, and their father eventually put a stop to them playing with hard balls. Around 30 windows had been broken and the insurance premiums had soared.

Luckily, there were a few options when it came to replacement balls. A grapefruit tree in the backyard proved handy. The unripe fruit were small enough and hard enough to keep the batsmen on their toes. As Allan recalled, 'They were as hard as any cricket ball, shiny and either skidded or bounced from the concrete slab, a true test of any batsman's technique.' Johnno Border reckons they were a good preparation for facing the West Indian quicks. 'They'd come out of the hand at 50 miles an hour and come off the concrete at 250 miles an hour. If you bowled a bouncer with them, well it was just the brothers trying to hit each other in the head.'

Ultimately grapefruit Test matches weren't sustainable. The Border brothers started playing with a stump and golf ball. Like in Don Bradman's backyard game in Bowral, the ball flew off the concrete, testing the reflexes and footwork of the batsman. Batting with a stump meant they had to learn to watch the ball right onto the bat. The balls were thrown, not bowled. Johnno, who ended up pitching for New South Wales in baseball, imparted wicked spin and bounce off the concrete pitch. 'Getting to the pitch of it was paramount,' Johnno recalls. 'I suppose it did have an influence, Allan's always been a good player of spin.' Border went on to be one of Australia's best players of the turning ball, scoring a series of big hundreds on the subcontinent. The boys also used plastic golf balls. 'They would swing and cut magnificently,' Johnno says. It seems like they had all bases covered when it came to practising against the moving ball.

Former England all-rounder Barry Knight, who had a big influence on Allan Border as a coach, says these formative years are critical. He told journalist Gideon Haigh, 'The way you play the game early has a big impact on what you do well later.' Knight himself was a consummate player of spin. His father built him a training pitch out of an old door after hearing that Len Hutton had learned to play on a wooden pitch. Knight's childhood training partner was a spinner who made the ball spit and kick off the planks that had been warped and distorted by the elements. When Knight started coaching Border he recognised that his home-grown technique had its benefits. 'The point is,' Border wrote, 'that Barry didn't try and change my natural style, he just tried to strengthen it.'

Allan Border always sold his wicket dearly. In Test cricket he remained undefeated 44 times – one out of every six times he batted. In 1984 at Port-of-Spain, he twice defied the fearsome West Indies attack, scoring 98 not out and 100 not out, to draw the match. Playing in the backyard at Mosman he was no kinder to the bowlers. 'It was probably harder to get him out in the backyard,' Johnno recalls. 'He didn't want to get out against Brett and me. We're a pretty close family, but there's nothing better than beating your brothers, there's no greater joy!' The backyard rules stated you had to retire at a hundred, and Allan often got there with a six over the back fence.

There was plenty of sledging as well. The worst accusation you could cop in the Border backyard was that you were chicken. In all their contests the boys played for keeps. One of their more brutal games involved darts. Unlike the conventional game of darts, where a board on the wall is the target, the brothers used each other as the bull's-eye. The target had to stand still and could only avoid the dart by swerving or ducking. If you moved your feet to get out of the way you were labelled a chicken. When the boys weren't hurling darts, or golf balls, or grapefruits, they played baseball. These games helped develop Allan's throwing arm, his eye and his strokes played with the horizontal bat.

If the Border boys wanted to play more expansive Test matches involving friends, they had a first-grade cricket ground at their disposal. Mosman Oval was right across the road. It was here the boys played what they called The Tornado Test of 1969. When a mini-tornado hit Mosman in 1969, most residents sought refuge in their homes. But not the Border boys, they had a match to finish. Allan recounted what happened in *Beyond Ten Thousand*.

'I was bowling to David Mankey. We were using a tennis ball because my little brother Brett, only eight years old and knee-high to a grasshopper, was playing. He was fielding at mid-on. I bowled the ball, and the wind caught it and swerved it back at me! David's startled look suddenly gave way to a cry, 'Hey look at Brett!' I turned to see little Brett wheeling towards me, airborne, picked up by the wind. I grabbed him by the legs, then lay on top of him. Might be the best catch I've ever made!'

While not even tornadoes could stop the Borders from playing cricket, sometimes wet weather got in the way. No drama there. They had that covered as well. A hallway inside had enough length and width to make a decent pitch. If the bowler wanted to come off the long run he ran in from the other side of the dining room. John Border, who originally came from Coonamble, must've gone against his bush instincts and prayed for dry weather. Three competitive boys playing indoor cricket in the family home would've been hard to control.

Even though Allan was playing most of his cricket against his younger brothers, he was able to test himself against older boys on weekends. As an eight-year-old he found himself playing in the Mosman under 12s. Because he was so good, the coaches wanted him to play above his age. At 12, he was playing under

14s. At 16, he made his debut in the Mosman first-grade side captain-coached by Barry Knight. Border later thanked Knight in his autobiography for the 'resuscitation job on my cricket career'. Knight, a veteran of 29 Tests and 279 first-class games, set up an indoor coaching school in a converted warehouse in Kent Street, Sydney. He combined old-school cricket know-how with modern technology. He was one of the first coaches to use video cameras. He filmed Allan batting in the nets and pointed out the areas he needed to work on.

Barry Knight helped develop the careers of a bunch of cricketers who went on to terrorise his former country, including the Waugh twins, Adam Gilchrist and Brett Lee. With Allan, he not only provided technical advice, he gave him a well-timed motivational talk. At the time, Border was also playing first-grade baseball for Mosman and his commitment to cricket was wavering. 'You're good enough to one day play cricket for your country,' Knight said to Border. 'Do you know what that means? It means the world is yours. Baseball can't offer you that.' Border practised hard throughout the winter of 1975 and within 18 months had made the New South Wales side. Right up to his selection in the Australian side, he used the backyard at Mosman for further practice. Johnno remembers him playing back and forward to a ball in a stocking. 'He'd probably hit it a thousand times a night, off the clothesline, or wherever he could hang it. Mum would often get up in the morning and have only one stocking.'

The backyard that cultivated Allan Border's home-grown technique is no longer suitable for playing cricket. The concrete slab that once acted as a pitch has been ripped up. Renovations have sucked up a large proportion of the backyard. A tiled deck and a pool have left only a very narrow strip of grass. It certainly isn't large enough to accommodate three boys who played in the vigorous style of the Border brothers. However a kid growing up in The Crescent today could still make use of the oval where the famous Tornado Test of 1969 was played. It's now called Allan Border Oval and continues to be the home of Mosman's first-grade cricket side.

Broken windows

While John Border was unlucky that his three sons played their backyard Tests within striking range of a block of flats, it could've been worse. He could've been Martin Chappell. While an estimated 30 windows were rearranged by the Border boys, the Chappell brothers are said to have hit the 150 mark. John Border paid his neighbours' insurance premiums, Martin Chappell struggled to find an insurer.

The Chappell brothers weren't just a danger to insurance premiums; they were a physical threat to the neighbours. One elderly woman narrowly avoided injury when the window pane came crashing in as she was doing her knitting. Another neighbour had his breakfast disturbed by a top-edged sweep shot from Greg. The ball smashed through the window onto his breakfast table before breaking his tomato sauce bottle and showering his face in sauce. Martin Chappell extended the height of the side fences to protect the neighbours' windows. When that didn't work, he repaired the windows himself.

Kids breaking windows with cricket balls has been going on for yonks. The 1927 silent film *The Kid Stakes* features a cricket game on a dirt pitch that turns into a romp through the streets of Woolloomooloo when a window gets broken. The film was based on the popular *Fatty Finn* comic strip of the day. Sid

Barnes, a real life street urchin of the same era, broke his fair share of windows in Stanmore. Barnes's grandfather George Jeffrey had his work cut out repairing his next-door neighbours' windows. So many off-drives went through their front window that it became a police matter. The boys responded by placing lookouts at deep point and deep square leg.

• • •

Young Lindsay Hassett, a future Australian captain and one of six boys, broke plenty of glass in his Geelong backyard. After the boys smashed a large window a number of times, they came up with the idea of fitting glass louvres. Repairing one glass louvre was easier and cheaper than fixing a whole window. The concept worked well until brother Dick accidentally let go of the stump he was using as a bat. The flying stump took out all the louvres at once.

• • •

Ashley Mallett and his brother Nick smashed a few glass louvres in their suburban backyard in Morley. 'Happily we discovered a few sheets of glass and a glass cutter,' Mallett recalls. 'With that we papered over our "mistakes" with bat or ball.' The Lee brothers found that prevention was better than cure in their backyard at Mt Warrigal. They covered the windows with boogie boards. Geoff Lawson learned the hard way not to play with a hard ball in his backyard at Wagga. The few times he broke the laundry window he had to pay for it out of his own pocket money.

• • •

But perhaps the last word belongs with Jeff Thomson, who was as carefree about breaking windows as he was about breaking batsmen's bones. The Thomson backyard pitch faced away from the kitchen window, making it a dangerous proposition when young Thommo was bowling. 'If somebody snicked it and Mum was doing dinner, you'd hear a scream then the glass went everywhere and we'd bolt,' Thomson told journalist David Brearley. 'One of the older brothers had to call the tradesman and get it fixed before dad got home. Never got the glass out of the dinner though.'

The TV Age
—Watching Tests, playing Tests and imitating your heroes

THE CRICKETERS WHO grew up in the 1970s and 1980s had the best of both worlds. They could watch Test matches in the living room and play Test matches in the backyard. Television coverage of cricket increased exponentially in the 1970s. World Series Cricket provided Supertests and one-day games. The ABC covered the traditional Tests. Even Sheffield Shield games were covered. While TV coverage was on the rise, the downsizing of backyards had yet to occur. Kids had the opportunities to play backyard cricket in the same way their Test cricket heroes had. The same could not be said 20 years later.

TV added an extra degree of authenticity to backyard Test matches. Saturation coverage meant you could mimic the styles of various players. If you were Dennis Lillee you leapt, appealed and snarled. If you were Allan Border you crouched in your stance. If you were Kim Hughes you charged down the wicket at everything.

Education went hand in hand with imitation. Ian Healy and Adam Gilchrist, though isolated from Test cricket in the country, were able to watch Rod Marsh keep wickets. The Waugh brothers could copy Thommo and bounce the hell out of each other. Shane Warne learned to appeal from Lillee. Mike Hussey became so obsessed with Allan Border that he swapped from right-handed to left-handed.

Ian Healy

PITCH: Grass pitch in backyard.

BAT: A Slazenger Polyarmour bat or a Gray Nicholls Terryarmour bat.

BALL: Tennis ball (and cricket balls when parents weren't looking).

WICKET: Rubbish bin.

PLAYERS: Ian and brothers Greg and Ken.

RULES: Mandarin tree automatic wicket-keeper, six and out. Hit the house or parts of the tree on the full and you were out.

HAZARDS: Willow-tree root sticking out of the pitch on a good length.

BACKYARD DRILLS: Ball in stocking drill.

PLAYERS' COMFORT LEVEL: Intense and hot. Central Queensland heat mixed in with plenty of attitude.

Ian Healy was one of the most competitive and passionate cricketers to represent his country. A durable and skilful keeper and peskily efficient number 7 batsman, he was like one of those tough but talented rugby league halfbacks from the 1970s.

Healy was always talking, always urging his team mates on. He rarely missed a chance and never took a backward step. Healy's tolerance of pain was legendary. His hands were described by one journalist as like 'the gnarled and broken claws of Macbeth's witches'. Despite all those broken fingers, he missed only one Test match in 11 years.

Greg Chappell recognised the toughness early on. He was one of the selectors who picked Healy to play for Australia after just six first-class matches. Chappell saw him as the kind of player who could help the Australian team rebuild under the leadership of those other hard nuts, Allan Border, David Boon and Geoff Marsh. The former Australian captain thought boys from the bush were tougher than their city counterparts because they had to compete against men from a young age. As Chappell explained to Healy's hometown newspaper, 'They get a bit of attention verbally and their character is put to the test.'

Healy's character was put to the test early on in the backyard. 'The advantage Ian had was he played against older people from day one,' his brother Greg says. 'I'm five years older than him and he was playing against blokes five years older than him since the age of four. So all the tricks you used in the backyard, where older guys would take advantage of him, he'd use those tricks in games. He was just tough.'

Most of those early games were played in Biloela, a small country town 600 kilometres north-west of Brisbane. When Ian was seven, his father, Neville, was sent north by the ANZ bank, a move that helped his son play for Australia. Ian Healy thinks he would not have been as good a cricketer if he'd spent those formative years in Brisbane. In Biloela he had the primary school nets across the road and could cycle around the playing fields trying to get a game with the seniors on a weekend. In

Biloela he got constant exposure to tough cricket, both in men's competitions and in the backyard.

The backyard at 40 Gladstone Road proved the perfect environment to develop combative cricketers. The pitch was on the back lawn. A spiky mandarin tree acted as the automatic wicketkeeper. At shortish mid-wicket was a weeping willow. The tree's roots ran across the pitch on a good length. The boys aimed at the roots and tried to knock each other's heads off. This competitive environment proved a good hothouse for the brothers' talents. All three Healy boys, Greg, Ian and Ken, went on to represent Queensland in the under 19s and play first-grade in Brisbane.

Disputes were commonplace, as Greg Healy recalls, 'The arguments would start if you nicked one. You were out, but no one ever walked. Mum would sit in the sewing room and would come out and break up the disputes. LBWs were in the game too, but they were always confrontational. But what would happen was your parents would side with the young one, but all that did was fire me up, and I would bring out the hard ball and aim at the tree root.' It's easy to imagine that the same Ian Healy, who irritated Desmond Haynes and Arjuna Ranatunga, was just as happy firing up his older brother.

While the Healy boys were not allowed to play with a hard ball, it came out when the parents weren't around, or to sort out umpiring disputes. This could lead to further trouble. If the ball hit the tree root at pace, it could take off like one of Jeff Thomson's rearing deliveries. Neville Healy knew what his boys were like, and grew a hedge over the fence to provide some insurance. But it wasn't quite high enough. During one weekend Test match the ball flew off the tree root, over the fence, through the window and onto the neighbours' dining table while they were having lunch. The home was owned by Mr Gesler, a rival bank manager. To his credit he didn't complain and in later years boasted that Ian Healy broke his window.

The backyard games at Gladstone Road were played like real Test matches, mimicking the contests of the mid 1970s when Ian Chappell's Australians terrorised other Test teams. Greg, as eldest brother, was most often Australia. Ian would be stuck with England or one of the other opposition teams. They batted one to eleven through the Test teams of the day, and if a left-handed batsman like John Edrich was in, they had to bat left-handed. Runs and wickets were entered in the scoresheets in the back of the annual ABC Cricket Book. Ian believes the authenticity of these games helped his cricket. 'It was just fantastic, that's where dreams begin, I suppose. You've got images in your mind you're trying to replicate. It doesn't ensure you will make it, but it stands you in good stead because when you make it, you do feel as if you've been there before.'

Greg Healy believes playing against older boys in the backyard environment was crucial for developing Ian's self belief: 'I think the backyard games made him think if I can do it there, why can't I do it anywhere else?' Ian Healy agrees these formative years were critical, 'Absolutely essential, no question, without it you don't make it. Kids have to spend time learning how to compete, learning how to win and lose, learning how to practise different things and cementing all their techniques before they hit a formal coach.'

When Ian didn't have his brothers to play with he found other ways to practise his skills. To work on his batting he put a cricket ball in one of his mum's stockings and hit it repeatedly as it dangled from the clothesline. As a Test cricketer he continued doing practice drills on his own. It was not uncommon to find

Healy in a hotel car park before a Test match throwing a golf ball against the wall to get his hands and feet moving properly.

Across the road from the family home in Gladstone Rd, the primary school nets got a good work out too. Ian often got together with mates from school to practise. The boys tried to hit the ball into the nearby hospital windows. Healy believes country kids have a big advantage over their city counterparts, 'I've noticed since my kids have grown up in the city how hard it is and how much city kids miss out on. It's so difficult to get them with their mates. They all come from different areas of the city to go to their schools, and then it's difficult to keep them together and difficult to get them to cricket nets and facilities. It was a big advantage for me being in the country.'

From the age of 11, Healy tried to get a game in the Biloela men's competition. Every Saturday and Sunday he hopped on his bike and called in on the town's three cricket ovals to see if one of the sides was short a player. If he got a game he batted at 11 and fielded fine leg to fine leg. On one occasion he stayed at the crease a little too long and Merv Bidgood, a grazier from Baralaba, tried to dislodge him by bouncing him. 'It was good for me,' Healy explained in *The Ian Healy Story: Playing for Keeps*: '... being tested and baked in an oven a little warmer than schoolboy cricket. It was not the last time in life I would be pitched into battle ahead of schedule.'

Riding from field to field looking for a game was typical of Healy's attitude and initiative. 'He didn't take anything for granted,' says brother Greg. 'He never had a free run at anything.' His mum Rae made his first set of pads and he saved up for his first bat through collecting bottles at football games during the winter of 1974. Still short of funds when the cricket season came round, Rae Healy put him on an incentive scheme: 5 cents for every run past 50, and 10 cents for every run after 100. Early in the season, he hit pay dirt scoring 179 against a team from Monto, securing enough funds for a new bat. Healy became one of those batsmen who scored runs when you needed them.

Ian Healy played cricket whenever he could throughout summer. He played informal games in the backyard and the nets. He got a run in men's games when he could snag one. He played for his primary school, in junior teams and in representative teams. Cricket was strong in Biloela in the 1970s. The town of around 5000 was able to sustain six competitive junior teams in Healy's age division throughout his time there. It provided competition and a structure from which he could progress to the top.

Sadly the cricket culture in Biloela that fostered Ian Healy's passion and dedication has diminished. While there's still plenty of big backyards and open space in Biloela, competitive cricket is dying in the town. In season 2008/9 only 45 kids from the ages of 7 to 14 were registered to play. In Healy's day there would've been more than 45 playing in just one age group. The juniors don't even play on Saturdays anymore. Instead the kids get together and have a hit on Friday nights. This is apparently a product of parents being unwilling to commit their children to a few hours of cricket on a Saturday. As Brett Hanson, President of the Biloela Juniors, puts it, 'Friday night cricket frees up families for the weekends.'

Marc McMahon, a former President of Biloela Juniors, says other sports are putting pressure on cricket. 'Soccer training starts in February and it overlaps with cricket. Their coaches tell them to choose between soccer and cricket.' One wonders at the logic of this argument. If Elysse Perry can continue to play cricket and soccer for Australia, presumably kids in Biloela could manage to play summer and winter sport. But it doesn't end there. There's not even an inter-school cricket competition in the area anymore. The local schools have rugby league teams and soccer teams, but no cricket teams. Within 30 years the culture that helped Ian Healy progress from bush cricketer to Test cricketer has disappeared. If it continues in other country towns, Australian cricket could be in trouble.

The Waugh Brothers

PITCH: Concrete driveway or front lawn.

BAT: Cricket bat, stump or fence paling.

BALL: Taped tennis ball. If they ran out of tennis balls, they taped a piece of foam up into a ball.

WICKET: Garage door.

PLAYERS: Brothers Steve, Mark, Dean and Danny.

RULES: Automatic wicketkeeper. Hitting stationary objects on the off side on the full (for example, the clothesline) was out. Moveable fielders (e.g. scooters or toys) were also out on the full.

HAZARDS: Each other.

BACKYARD DRILLS: Ball in stocking.

PLAYERS' COMFORT LEVEL: Intensely competitive. Lots of bouncers. Game could descend into fights or brandings.

The backyard at 56 Picnic Point, Panania, was the perfect 1970s environment for cultivating Test cricketers. Steve and Mark Waugh had in each other the ideal training companions; same age, same competitive spirit, same skill base, same thirst for constant play. There was no wandering the neighbourhood looking for a hit or waiting on a friend to come over. From the time school finished it was game on. Sibling rivalry makes backyard cricket intense at the best of times. Mix that in with the competitive nature of twins, who spend their whole lives being compared, and you create an environment of extreme competition.

The Waugh boys were born into a strong sporting culture. Rodger and Bev Waugh were both junior tennis champions. Rodger won the New South Wales under 14 Grass Court Championship. Bev took out the South Australian under 14 title. Bev's brother, Dion Bourne, was captain of Bankstown's first XI, where he still holds the record for most runs. Bev was 19 and Rodger was 20 when the twins were born, young and active enough to play competitively with their kids, and to continue playing tennis tournaments. While Bev and Rodger were on the court, the boys would throw balls at each other. 'They were coordinated when they were really young,' Bev recalled in *Waugh Declared*, '18 months old catching balls and connecting with balls, I always thought unless something went drastically wrong they were going to reach the top level.'

Panania, a working class suburb in south-west Sydney, was a good place to foster such talent. The Bankstown area has good sporting facilities and a tough sporting culture. The region has produced a range of characters with a hunger for the contest, including Jeff Thomson, Len Pascoe, Terry Lamb, Ian Thorpe and Paul Keating. Panania in the 1970s was a suburb stacked with fibro homes on quarter-acre blocks. Lawns and driveways were filled with young boys trying to imitate their heroes of the day, in particular Dennis Lillee, Jeff Thomson, Rod Marsh and the Chappell brothers.

The Waughs played most of their backyard cricket on a concrete driveway that ran along the side of the house. It sloped down towards the batsman, giving the bowler an advantage. The garage door fulfilled multiple roles as the wicket, backstop and automatic wicketkeeper. On the off side imaginary fielders were scattered everywhere. If you hit any of the stationary objects, like the clothesline, on the full, you were out. Scooters, toys and other moveable objects were strategically placed in other fielding positions. On the leg side there was not much on due to vines and other plants covering the side fence. Maybe this explains Steve's reluctance to play the hook shot in later years.

The front lawn provided an alternate pitch with a whole different set of conditions. Here the slope ran across the pitch, and the batsman had to deal with wicked off-cutters. 'The front yard offered a real test of hand–eye coordination for the batsman,' Steve wrote in *Out of My Comfort Zone*. 'You had to counteract this excessive sideways movement by going with the angle and flicking it off the stumps in direction of midwicket. This shot ended up being Mark's trademark stroke, and would also prove a productive area for me throughout my career.'

The Waugh brothers did themselves a favour by making their backyard games difficult for batsmen. Surviving for a long period with the bat in hand was quite a task. It wasn't just the slopes on pitches, the multiple 'fieldsmen' and the combative bowlers you had to deal with. The ball, taped heavily on one side, swung all over the shop. Sometimes the fur was shaved off the tennis ball for the same purpose. At times the brothers forced each other to bat with a stump, or a fence paling or a small child's bat just to make conditions even more difficult. These weren't flat-track bullies used to cruising in the best of conditions. They had to fight for survival in a game situation where the bowler had the upper hand.

Unsurprisingly, there were plenty of bouncers bowled. Mark and Steve would do anything to win. 'We had to get the bat out of each other's hands.' Steve recalled in *Waugh Declared*. 'The tendency to bowl a few short ones, that stems from our backyard cricket. We were always trying to knock each other's head off.' In his first Test against the West Indies, Steve bounced their captain Viv Richards three times in a row. This was at a time when Richards had Marshall, Ambrose, Patterson and Walsh to call on, on a fast deck. It was an early sign that Steve would refuse to be intimidated by the West Indies fast men. It wasn't just their opponents that the Waugh twins enjoyed getting stuck into. As their former skipper Geoff Lawson recalled, 'At training sessions, both Waugh brothers found it amusing to hit less accomplished lower-order players.'

About the only civilised aspect of the Waugh brothers' backyard games came at the start of their matches, and that only lasted a few seconds. They would toss the bat to see who was Australia and who was England, and get on with it. If the batsman was hit by a short-pitched delivery they often chucked it back just as fast at the bowler. The match invariably descended into a game of brandings. As Steve recalled, 'One of us would wet the ball so it would sting a bit more.' Good practice for getting used to the feel of facing Allan Donald or Curtly Ambrose. It must've been a tough environment for their younger brothers Dean (four years younger) and Danny (ten years younger) to venture into. In some ways it's a surprise they didn't take up something more sedate. But Dean went on to play for New South Wales, while Danny won the Benaud Medal in 2003 for best player in the Sydney first-grade final.

The competitive instincts of the twins are perhaps best summed up by a non-cricketing story. Steve and Mark used to have scooter races down the driveway. They started at the road and flew down the driveway, swinging left between the house and the garage, before finishing up at the clothesline. To win the race it was critical to get the inside running on the bend. On one occasion, Steve was looking good. He had a rails run, but was worried Mark was about to take him on the outside. He kicked out with his right leg and connected with Mark's ankle. 'For a split second and for the first time, I saw genuine fear on Mark's face,' Steve wrote, 'and for good reason, as he slammed into the painted diamond on the garage's timber door.' Mark was injured slightly, and his scooter was a wreck, but Steve won, which was the most important thing.

Despite this overwhelming competitive streak, the boys struggled in their first game of competition cricket. Playing for the Panania-East Hills RSL under 10s, they lasted only three balls between them. But they were playing against boys three years older than them. Nevertheless, they soon caught up with their older opponents and team mates. Brian Freedman, long time President of Bankstown Cricket Club, saw them play in those early days, 'They were much better than any other kid, they could catch like no other, their running between the wickets, they just had that basic understanding. They were just very special from the early stage.'

One of the things that made them special was the instinctive way they played. The Waugh brothers were pretty much self-taught in the backyard at Panania. 'We had a bit of coaching but nothing that changed anything,' said Mark. 'We just watched cricket on TV and just developed our own game. We never copied anyone. It's just a natural thing.' When the boys went and saw

Barry Knight at his indoor coaching centre he told them they were naturals and they should keep doing what they were doing. Their uncle Dion Bourne, who was captaining Bankstown's first-grade side at the time, thought they didn't need any intervention from him. Australian fast bowler Len Pascoe, who went on to coach New South Wales, had one look at them as 13 to 14 year olds and said he couldn't teach them anything.

The Waugh brothers weren't just naturals at cricket. They could play any ball sport with ease. By the age of 12, they'd represented New South Wales at cricket, tennis and soccer. As biographer Jack Egan points out, these other sports helped complement their cricket skills. 'If you wanted to pick two sports to play that would help you become a good cricketer, it would be hard to choose better than tennis, with its emphasis on placement and hand–eye coordination, and soccer, where the essentials are balance and footwork.' Other great bats like Don Bradman, Arthur Morris, and Belinda Clark also played a lot of tennis as youngsters.

When it was too dark or too wet to play in the Waugh backyard, or miraculously, they couldn't find anyone else to play with, both Mark and Steve practised their batting alone. They put a ball in one of Bev's stockings, threw it over the beam in the garage, and hit the ball for hours. Steve has no doubt this backyard drill had a big impact on his development. 'I believe I learnt patience and perseverance from the thousands of hours I spent alone in the garage,' he wrote. 'Without knowing it, I was enthusiastically searching for the perfect technique and developing routines that would later form the basis around which my game could evolve.'

The backyard Tests at Panania were crucial in helping Steve and Mark develop their skills and their ability to compete. As

Steve wrote, 'Duelling with Mark, Dean and Danny over the years provided a perfect learning environment for the battles that lay ahead.' So, what if a group of cricket mad brothers were growing up in Panania today? Would they have the same space and opportunities to fulfil their potential? A few of the old quarter-acre blocks in the area have lost their backyards after being redeveloped into duplexes. But in the main the backyards of Panania have been left alone, for now at least.

In the vicinity of the Waugh family's old home in Picnic Point Road, there's a string of houses with driveways as long as the Nullarbor. These places are made for playing backyard cricket. There seems to be plenty of kids in the area signed up to play junior cricket. Panania-East Hills RSL has even more junior teams now than they did when the Waugh boys played for them in the 1970s. But would these kids play as hard and as often as the Waugh brothers? It's hard to imagine children today, with their thirst for video games, clocking up as many hours in the backyard as Steve and Mark.

It would certainly be harder to do so at 56 Picnic Point Road. The garage that was used by the Waugh boys for their ball in the stocking drill, and as a backstop and automatic wicketkeeper has been demolished. In its place is a swimming pool. You could still play on the driveway, but anything past the batsman would end up in the water. On a hot summer's day in Sydney's west it might be hard to get out of that pool once you retrieved the ball.

Belinda Clark

PITCH: Concrete driveway in backyard and concrete footpath opposite local pool.

BAT: Normal bat in backyard, and thin bat for games near the pool.

BALL: Tennis ball for games (sometimes taped), cricket ball for fielding.

WICKET: Metal stumps.

PLAYERS: Belinda, brother Colin, father Alan, and boys across the road.

RULES: Automatic wicketkeeper, out if you hit the cars outside the pool, in the drain was four, past Kemp Street was four.

HAZARDS: Loose stones on the driveway run up, could lose a bit of skin taking catches on the concrete, would have to avoid cars flying past in Kemp Street, moss, glass and gunk in the stormwater drain.

BACKYARD DRILLS: Classic catches over the clothesline, throwing against the wall, batting against the garage door.

PLAYERS' COMFORT LEVEL: Challenging. Always playing against older, competitive boys.

Belinda Clark was around three years old when she first got a taste for cricket. It was late on a summer's afternoon at Spring Ridge Public School, west of Werris Creek in country New South Wales. Belinda's father Alan, the local school principal, was throwing balls at his eldest son Colin in the school nets. Belinda stood behind her brother, separated by the wire fencing, soaking it all in. When Colin finished his session, Belinda walked around to the front of the nets, picked up the bat and refused to leave till she was thrown some balls. With a pad strapped to her front leg that was nudging her armpit, she took guard and started batting.

By the age of four, Belinda was getting a regular hit. By then, the sports mad family of six had moved to Hamilton South, a suburb of Newcastle. Each night Belinda eagerly awaited the completion of ABC TV's 7 pm news. It was then that Dad came out the back and started bowling. Colin batted first; Belinda faced up in the fading light. Getting used to the most difficult of batting conditions was good training for a future Test opener.

If it wasn't for daylight saving, Belinda might have struggled to get a bat. Without the introduction of Eastern Summer Time, it would've been pitch dark by the time James Dibble completed his news bulletin. In 1971, the New South Wales government passed a law that saw the clocks wound forward during the summer months. A referendum in 1976 made it permanent. Although it upset farmers and Queenslanders, it gave the Clarks and many other kids in New South Wales an extra hour of backyard cricket each night.

The Clark family home at 6 Jenner Parade had a solid backyard pitch. A flat concrete driveway ran down the side of the house, leading to a turning circle and double garage down the back. The driveway acted as a run-up; the bowler then darted around the corner and delivered the ball onto the concrete strip. The old wooden garage door took a pounding. In backyard Tests it was the automatic wicketkeeper and backstop. When no one else was around to take on, tennis balls were thumped against it for hours on end.

Colin Clark was five years older than Belinda. He gained experience from formal coaching and competition games and was able to pass his skills on to Belinda in the backyard. By playing against an older, stronger opponent Belinda learned how to tough it out, the cornerstone of any good opener's game. 'When you play with younger people you're probably more expansive in what you're trying to do because you're not worried about getting out,' Clark says, 'whereas when you're playing against older people, there's this survival mechanism which is there from the beginning.'

Like most Australian backyard Tests, these games were played for keeps. 'I didn't back off,' Colin recalls. 'She was wanting to beat me, and that could never happen!' Colin wasn't completely remorseless. He'd slip in the quick yorker rather than the bouncer to dislodge his gutsy younger sister. Once Colin was batting, Belinda would do anything to get him out. 'If there was a catch to be taken and it meant taking some skin off the elbows on the driveway, she would take it,' Colin says. 'She was always relentless about doing the best she could.'

The Clark family took their sport seriously. Belinda's mum Margaret and elder sister, Sally, both won Newcastle tennis championships. Colin played first-grade cricket and was a handy footballer and surfer. Her younger sister Helen also played tennis competitively. Belinda Clark has no doubt being exposed to strong competition at an early age helped her later in her career. 'If you're always playing where there are sheep stations on the line you tend not to worry about it later on. Whereas people who are in an incubator type of upbringing, or always in programs, they tend not to have that ability to withstand the pressure.' Pressure didn't seem to be a problem in Belinda's first Test match. At the age of 20, she scored a century on debut.

The back wall of the house in Jenner Parade was used for fielding practice. Belinda drew a set of stumps on the wall. With chalk she marked her target zone on the brick above the bails. The thud of leather on brick was not music to the ears of other family members. Belinda was banned from doing it when anyone else was at home. 'I could spend hours playing by myself with a ball and a wall and I did so,' Clark recalled. She did it so often and with such accuracy that the brick dislodged and started to move into the house. Catching practice was less damaging to the family home. The ball was thrown over the clothesline with diving chances taken on the other side of the Hills Hoist, mimicking Channel Nine's 'Classic Catches' contests of the day.

As Colin Clark got older and the backyard games dried up, Belinda drifted across the road and played cricket in the street with Troy Arnold and Geoff Cooke. Both boys were two years older than Belinda and would go on to play first-grade cricket. Troy was the son of the local swimming pool owner and they played their Tests on a concrete footpath between the pool and the road. Each player rotated on dismissal, from batter to fielder to bowler. They used a skinny bat and a taped-up tennis ball that hooped in the air. Any shot that hit any of the cars owned by clients of the swimming pool was automatically out. There was a strong incentive to stay in. If you were fielding you were placed on the leg side in Kemp Street and had to dodge cars. Straight hits had to be retrieved from the local stormwater drain which was full of water, moss and broken bottles.

While Belinda Clark became obsessed with cricket, tennis was her first true sporting love. She stayed up late and watched the Wimbledon finals in the late 1970s and early 1980s. These were epic contests, such as Borg vs McEnroe and Evert vs Navratilova. Belinda played a lot of tennis as a child and believes this had a huge influence on her cricket. 'When you went to tennis squad, if you were there for two hours, you probably spent an hour forty-five of that hitting balls yourself.' At most cricket training sessions you're lucky if you bat for 15 minutes. Through tennis practice she was able to work on her footwork, fitness and hand–eye coordination at a more intense level.

Even when her younger sister was at tennis practice, Belinda found a way to work on her cricket shots. When Helen was hitting balls Belinda placed herself on the other side of the net and tried to deflect the balls into the bucket as if she was playing a leg-glance. 'Having a racquet in my hand from an early age I could play drop shots and hit top spin and slice. When I put a cricket bat in my hand I could understand the deflections. I could take the pace off the ball and those sorts of things.'

Tennis remained Belinda's main game until she was around 14. Attending Newcastle High, where they had a girls' cricket team, proved a turning point. At school she represented the region in tennis, hockey and cricket. All three sports helped her practise hitting a moving ball. Clark believes country towns provide young people with more options when it comes to playing sport. 'You're not as dependent on parents to get you around so therefore you can try lots of different sports,' Clark argues. Belinda and her siblings rode their bikes to training and games. Often their parents were playing sport themselves, so they had to take responsibility for getting themselves to games.

While Newcastle High had a girls' cricket team, there was

no local girls' team to play for on weekends. Being used to the rough and tumble of games with her brother in the backyard and the boys across the road, Belinda signed up to play with the Newcastle City boys under 16s team. The team included Anthony Stuart who ended up taking a hat-trick for Australia in a one-day international. Playing first division cricket against boys who were a year older was a tough experience. 'I remember my first run,' Belinda recalls. 'It was a beautiful French cut one day in about week 6 of the competition.'

Playing as a fourteen-year-old girl against young men on bouncy astroturf pitches was a gutsy move. But Clark learned some crucial lessons from the experience, that 'If you stick to some pretty basic stuff you can still succeed without being brilliant. There are some quite fundamental things in cricket you need to be able to do, if you can do them, you may not score a lot of runs, but you'll be able to survive and often that was all I was trying to do.' Many of Australia's best women cricketers have come from country areas where they had to play in the local boys' competitions.

Clark was a beneficiary of the indoor cricket revolution that swept Australia in the 1980s. The local Howzat Sports Centre opened in 1984, and before long she was playing in women's and mixed competitions. It was here she met Sally Griffiths, a future Australian Test player who introduced Clark to Sydney grade cricket, and Martin Soper, a coach who worked on her technique. Not that it needed much finessing. 'She had a much better technique than anyone I'd ever coached before,' Soper said. 'I'd coached a lot of first-grade male players, and she had more talent than all of them put together.' She also had a strong work ethic. Soper got Clark to face as many deliveries as she could in the indoor nets. Clark worked away at her strokes until she felt they were as close to perfection as they could be. Her Australian coach John Harmer later described her as technically 'the best player in the world, man or woman'. By the time she retired, she held the record for most runs by an Australian woman in Test matches and one-day internationals. Her average in Tests was 45.95. In one-dayers it was 47.49.

So what of an aspiring young female cricketer growing up in Newcastle now? Well, the conditions haven't changed much. The Hunter region remains a haven for sport. There are plenty of playing fields and organised sport, but still no girls' cricket competition. They do have junior representative teams, but the girls have to play their club cricket with the boys. The lie of the land in Jenner Street is pretty similar as well. The strip outside the pool is still ripe for a game of street cricket. Across the road at the Clarks' old house, the concrete backyard pitch is still in order. The old wooden garage door, terrorised by the Clark siblings in the 1970s and 1980s, is still hanging in there. There's no sign of displaced bricks in the backyard though. The brick wall that was hammered by Belinda's fielding drills has been rendered. The pock-marked brick at stump-height, a symbol of the kind of obsessive practice it takes to get you to the top, has been covered over.

Glenn McGrath

PITCH: Dirt pitch behind Dad's machinery shed.

BAT: Normal cricket bat.

BALL: Cricket ball.

WICKET: Upturned water trough or 44-gallon fuel drum.

PLAYERS: Early days, Glenn, brother Dale, sister Donna, cousin Craig. In later years Glenn played by himself.

HAZARDS: Pitch full of pebbles and divots.

BACKYARD DRILLS: Bowling at fuel drum, throwing rocks at rabbits and foxes.

PLAYERS' COMFORT LEVEL: Hot and exhausting work bowling at the fuel drum after labouring on the farm.

On a dirt pitch under a hot sun on a bush property west of Dubbo, one of Australia's greatest ever quicks learned to love bowling. In such conditions most people would learn to love getting horizontal. Finding some shade, a cool drink and a banana lounge seems the most sensible option in the oppressive heat of

Narromine's searing summers. Instead, Glenn McGrath set up a makeshift pitch out the back of his Dad's machinery shed and worked away at cricket's most labour-intensive art form.

The young Glenn McGrath had no reason to love bowling fast. He wasn't particularly good at it. Family members recall younger sister, Donna, as being the standout bowler in their backyard games. This may be the McGrath family's bush humour coming to the fore, but there was a grain of truth to it. In the Backwater under 16s, Glenn struggled to get a bowl. Captain Shane Horsborough threw him the ball as a fifth or sixth change if he was lucky. His skipper used to say 'a broomstick had more ability'. As Mark Munro, the team's gun bowler recalled, 'Glenn was just too erratic'.

It seems inconceivable that the teenaged McGrath dreamed of playing cricket for Australia. Opening the bowling for one of the junior teams in a town with less than 4000 people may have been a more realistic goal. But even then McGrath had extraordinary self-belief. Critical to his dream was his training ritual on the strip near his Dad's shed. He placed an old 44-gallon drum at one end and paced out 22 yards. The pitch, McGrath recalled, was 'pockmarked with pebbles and deep divots'. But each evening, after helping on the farm, he picked up a worn-out old cricket ball and pegged away at that old fuel drum, imagining he was bowling in a Test match for Australia. 'I firmly believe,' McGrath wrote, 'it is because I had to work much harder than the next bloke to get any scrap of recognition as a kid that I achieved my goal of playing for Australia.'

The best fast bowlers are born leaders. When they have the ball in their hands, they inspire team mates and make opposition players nervous. At a young age, Glenn had to assume a lot of responsibility. When he was 16, his father had to take up long-haul truck driving to earn some extra money. Glenn and his younger brother Dale had to sow and harvest wheat across the 1140-acre property while their father was away. It placed a lot of pressure on the boys – their family's livelihood depended on their ability to get the job done. 'We were kids doing men's work,' McGrath wrote, '… nothing I've done as a cricketer has matched the tiredness I felt back then!' Exhausted after his work on the farm, McGrath still managed to squeeze in some bowling before dusk. It was the perfect training for a Test bowler in the making. How a quickie responds in their third and fourth spell at the end of a long hard day is critical to their team's fortunes.

McGrath built up his strength and stamina through hard, energy-sapping work. Not only did he help his father out on the farm, he worked in a number of manual jobs after quitting school in Year 10. He dug fence posts, picked cotton, ploughed fields and worked as a labourer, sometimes for as many as 70 hours a week. Like fellow bush quick, Alan Davidson, he eventually found less strenuous work in a bank. But there's no doubt his upbringing helped develop his stamina and determination. He was able to bowl consistently long spells over a career spanning nearly 15 years. Most Australian quicks don't make it past 50 Tests. Lindwall played 61 Tests, Lillee 70, McDermott and Gillespie 71, Lee 76. McGrath kept going for 124.

Like other fine bush cricketers, such as Bradman and O'Reilly, McGrath was largely self-taught. While he was able to watch a golden era of quicks in action on television – Marshall, Garner, Roberts, Holding, Hadlee, Imran Khan, Thomson and Lillee – he never tried to copy any of their individual styles. He acquired one of the most natural actions in world cricket. As McGrath says, 'My body found its most natural way to bowl and I'm sure that is what allowed me to enjoy longevity.' His action was front-on, and his hips and shoulders were in alignment, helping him avoid the kind of injuries that Brett Lee and Jason Gillespie suffered.

The simplicity of his home-grown style helped with his consistency as well. A straightforward action has fewer areas where it can go wrong. When McGrath went to the Cricket Academy, Rod Marsh thought it was one of the most natural fast bowling actions he'd seen. McGrath saw his lack of coaching as a youngster as an advantage. 'As a kid I was always desperate to be given some direction at my team's training sessions,' he wrote in *Pacemaker* in 1998,' but now I've established myself as a first-class cricketer I'm eternally grateful no one took me under their wing!'

While Glenn didn't have much in the way of coaching at Narromine, he was fortunate to come in contact with Brian Gainsford, a former representative cricketer who became the Chairman of the New South Wales Country Cricket Association. At the age of 17, McGrath wasn't sure if he should stick at cricket or toss it in and play basketball. After a game, he sought out Gainsford for a chat. 'I told him that regardless of whether he played in the bush or went all the way to become an international cricketer, he'd make great friends,' Gainsford recalls. After their hour-long discussion, McGrath worked even harder at his bowling behind the machinery shed. He started making small steps, bowling more for his club side, and getting selected for local representative teams.

At 18, McGrath got his big opportunity. Gainsford was one of the selectors who picked him in the Dubbo team to play Parkes in the Tooheys Country Cup Challenge. The competition, inspired by Jack Chegwyn's country tours of the 1940s, 1950s and 1960s brought first-class cricketers to the bush to play alongside talented country players. It was a way to identify the best cricketers from around New South Wales. McGrath came on first change and bowled to Doug Walters, who himself was discovered in one of Jack Chegwyn's games in Maitland in 1962. Bowling under lights at Pioneer Oval, Parkes, McGrath had Walters dropped in the gully early on. Walters was so impressed by his performance he got his phone number after the game and passed it on to the New South Wales coach Steve Rixon.

Rixon was another bush cricketer. Born in Albury, he played for Southern Riverina against England in 1970/71 as a 16-year-old. He invited McGrath down to play with his old club Sutherland for the 1989/90 season. McGrath bought a Millard caravan and with some help from his mum Bev, towed it on a seven-hour journey to the Grand Pines Tourist Park at Ramsgate, the cheapest caravan park in the vicinity of Caringbah Oval. As Bev drove away, leaving her 19 year-old boy alone in the big smoke for the first time, tears came to her eyes. Eight minutes after she left, Glenn grabbed a ball and a stump and headed to the nets across the road to practise on his own, just like on the family property. 'I'm adamant,' McGrath wrote, 'the time I spent toughing it out in the old Millard helped brace me for the strict discipline which is needed to survive in top-class cricket.' Thirteen months later he was out of the caravan park. Within four years he'd achieved his dream of playing for Australia.

So could another fast bowler with the talent and hunger of Glenn McGrath emerge from the same environment today? Cricketers raised in the country still have two advantages over their city counterparts – easier access to playing fields and open spaces, plus the physical and mental toughness a bush upbringing tends to give you. But in recent years the drought and changing work and economic circumstances have made playing sport in remote areas more difficult. Brian Gainsford says the smaller country villages with populations of around 500 to 1000, which used to sustain eight or nine teams, no longer have competitive cricket. In the bigger town centres like Narromine, with populations of 3000 to 5000, competitions are still in place but the quality and quantity of players has diminished.

The drought and rising petrol costs have put increased pressure on families in far west New South Wales. It's harder to drive children hundreds of kilometres to sporting carnivals. Many parents have taken up weekend work in mines to make a living. This has made it even harder to sustain competition within and between country regions. Brian Gainsford has noticed another factor as well. 'People are not as dedicated as they used to be. In my day, if you were dropped to second grade you'd work your butt off to make it back into firsts. That's not the case today, because there are so many sports, and I have a son involved in Sydney grade cricket and he says it's the same thing down there, where they can just say "Well if you drop me I will go and do something else ..." That toughness has gone out of a lot of cricketers, not just country cricketers.'

The Tooheys Country Cup Challenge, the competition that first showcased the talents of Glenn McGrath, no longer exists. But on the upside Brian Gainsford argues there's a better talent identification process now in place. Youth programs are run full-time by co-coordinators right around the state. This system identified Phillip Hughes, the son of a Macksville banana farmer who at 20 became the youngest player to score two centuries in a Test match. They also spotted Josh Hazlewood, a 197 centimetre tall quick from Bendemeer, who at 17 became the youngest fast bowler to play for New South Wales. Hazlewood's childhood hero was Glenn McGrath. While McGrath took 5/79 on debut, Hazlewood took 4/76 in his first game. Comparisons between the two are inevitably made, but already there's one big point of difference. 'I don't think I'll live in a caravan for a year,' Hazlewood says.

Adam Gilchrist

PITCH: Front lawn at Deniliquin, astroturf pitch in the backyard at Goonellabah.

BAT: First bat – a cut-down Slazenger.

BALL: Tennis balls, cricket balls, golf balls.

PLAYERS: Adam, brothers Dean and Glenn, sister Jacki, mother June, father Stan, and neighbours.

BACKYARD DRILLS: Hitting golf balls with a stump, using thin bats and heavy bats. Forearm curls with a home-made device.

PLAYERS' COMFORT LEVEL: Tough competition against older siblings, relentless drills in the backyard nets.

It's hard to imagine a more natural striker of a cricket ball than Adam Gilchrist. When you consider his upbringing, it's little wonder that belting balls comes so instinctively. A sawn-off Slazenger was first placed in his hands at the age of two. Every morning, after June Gilchrist had made the lunches and got her older children off to school, it was time to warm up her throwing arm. While most pre-school kids move restlessly from one activity to another, all Adam wanted to do was play cricket. June had to toss balls at young Adam for hours on end. 'He was insatiable,' says his father Stan.

Adam Gilchrist was born into a strong cricketing culture. His father made the New South Wales squad as a leg-spinner and dismissed South African legends Graeme Pollock and Colin Bland while playing for Australian Universities. All three of Adam's siblings played cricket at a competitive level. Jacki became the first woman to play in the Deniliquin men's competition. Dean played for New South Wales under 17s. Glenn was gifted at a range of sports.

The Gilchrist children had to acclimatise to a few different backyard pitches around country New South Wales, in Junee, Deniliquin and Goonellabah. It was in Junee, 50 kilometres south-west of Bradman's birthplace in Cootamundra, that Adam first put bat on ball. By the time the family shifted to Deniliquin when he was around seven, backyard cricket was a big part of his life.

In Henry Street, Deniliquin, they played their Tests on the large nature strip outside the Jefferies home next door. The Jefferies family, like the Gilchrists, had three boys and one girl. Two of the Jefferies boys went on to play first-grade cricket in Melbourne, so the standard on both sides was high. The facilities weren't bad either. Ray Jefferies was a greenkeeper at the local golf club and kept an immaculate front lawn. One day, Adam was caught practising out the front of the Jefferies' place by Mrs Jorgensen, the secretary of the local primary school. 'Why aren't you playing on your own nature strip?' she called out. 'Mrs Jorgensen,' Adam replied, 'If I'm going to play for Australia I need the best wickets possible.'

As the youngest of four siblings, Adam was exposed to a

heightened level of competition. 'Even though I was the youngest,' he wrote in *True Colours: My Life*, 'I always thought I ought to be able to do the same things as them, to compete at the same level. What did I care about age difference? Because they were so talented, I was unwittingly setting standards for myself that were years ahead of my age.' His development was further fast-tracked when he started playing A-grade cricket in Lismore at the age of 14. That year he took a catch and a stumping off his father's bowling in the district final.

But Adam wasn't always destined to be a wicketkeeper. When he was nine, he was more interested in swing and seam. Terry Alderman had just taken 42 wickets in the 1981 Ashes series and became a source of inspiration. 'I loved his style,' Gilchrist wrote, 'How he ran in nice and easy, got side-on and swung the ball both ways, and in the backyard I'd be Terry Alderman, always.' But the mystical forces of impulse shopping soon put paid to that. When the family went to Shepparton for their annual Christmas shopping trip, Adam spied a pair of green and white wicket-keeping gloves in Kmart. Something told him he just had to have them.

Wicketkeepers are a tough breed. They routinely break fingers, thumbs and noses. Australia has been blessed with a long line of no-nonsense keepers with high pain thresholds. Men like Wally Grout, Rod Marsh and Ian Healy. Adam soon learned about the harsh realities of standing behind the stumps. The first time he wore his green and white gloves in a match, they turned a shade of red. When he was moving to gather a wayward return, the ball hit the edge of the concrete pitch and crashed into his face. He spent the night in hospital with a broken nose.

It could've ended badly. The boy who went on to be regarded as the greatest ever wicketkeeper/batsman could well have gone back to doing Terry Alderman impersonations in the backyard. Thankfully someone at the hospital told Adam the same thing had happened to Rod Marsh the first time he kept wickets. It wasn't true, but it gave him an instant connection with his latest cricketing hero. Rod Marsh later coached Adam at the Cricket Academy, and put him right about the story. Both played 96 Tests for their country, never missing a match through injury.

In 1984, the Gilchrists moved to Goonellabah. They lost the use of the highly manicured lawn outside the Jefferies' home, but were one step closer to the ultimate backyard cricket environment. When they first moved to the North Coast, Adam did most of his practising down at the local primary school nets. When they drove along the Ballina Cutting, a stretch of road between Alstonville and Ballina, the family passed a set of backyard practice nets. All the boys, Stan included, eyed those nets off with envy. Stan Gilchrist knew how good it was to have your own nets. He spent the first ten years of his life living in tents in Western Queensland where his father, Bill, made a living as a roo shooter and rabbit trapper. When the family settled down in Bukkulla, 30 kilometres north of Inverell, his Dad rolled a rough pitch out of ant's nests in the paddock next to the house. He then constructed a primitive set of nets out of chicken wire. Stan and his brother Jack were able to practise in the paddock without spending all their time chasing balls.

When Stan decided to build a backyard net in Goonellabah, it was a little more sophisticated. He landscaped a long, flat area by the side of the house and poured a concrete pitch. He bought some portable nets and draped them around the concrete. At first they laid some canvas down over the pitch to save the balls getting scuffed, but later replaced it with astroturf. Soon they added a bowling machine and a video camera. The Gilchrist backyard had evolved into a mini Cricket Academy. They even had the best local coach in residence. Stan had become the Regional Director of Cricket for the Far North Coast and was responsible for coaching the best young players in the area.

A lot of cricketers will have a weakness in their batting due to the layout of their childhood backyard. A rose bush, a set of windows, a favourite plant, even a cranky neighbour can stop you from playing certain shots. With a net in his backyard, Adam had no such restrictions. He could practise all his strokes at will. The ability to play around the ground became a prominent feature in his batting. Ian Healy saw it the first time he played him in a Sheffield Shield game. 'His ability to hit to all parts made him extremely difficult to bowl to,' Healy wrote. 'There was no black hole in his scoring range.'

Each afternoon, Adam got into the backyard net and batted for hours. If Stan wasn't around, June fed balls into the bowling machine. When Stan got back they worked on a series of batting drills. They used a sawn-off bat to work on shots played with the top hand; narrow bats to work on his eye; and heavy bats, with lead tape wrapped around them, to work on strength. Adam also used the Bradman backyard technique of hitting golf balls with a stump. Many of the drills were done at high speed to increase pressure. As Stan describes it, 'Almost so there's no time to recover, and then the next one is coming at you. So you're building pressure and teaching them how to cope with pressure.'

In 2007, Gilchrist became the first batsman to hit 100 sixes in Test cricket. Although not endowed with the body of a gym junkie, he does have very strong forearms and wrists. In the backyard at Goonellabah Stan set up a DIY arm strengthening exercise that helped him become one of the cleanest hitters in world cricket. They filled up old oil bottles with water, attached them to a length of cord, and tied it around an old broomstick. With the arms fully stretched out and hands on the broomstick, Adam would do forearm curls. 'I remember feeling this burn in the forearm,' he recalls, 'I did it in the morning, as soon as I woke up, and at night.'

Crucially each net session ended with 10 minutes of free hitting. Stan told his son to 'just hit the ball'. The idea evolved out of his time spent training with Richie Benaud. As Stan explains, 'When I went to Sydney I was fortunate enough to get into the state squad. Richie used to tutor me – how to bowl a wrong 'un, how to bowl a flipper, but he always said finish up the session with ten minutes of your stock leg-break so you'll never lose your leg-break. I developed the belief you could do all the technical training, practising and drills, all these things, but you need to finish up doing what you do naturally, and Adam hit the ball hard naturally.'

'Just hit the ball' became the key philosophy behind Adam's batting. No matter what the circumstances, if the ball was there to be hit, he walloped it. As the great Pakistani quick Wasim Akram put it, 'He can hit the first ball he faces, or the best ball you bowl, for a four.' Wasim Akram would know. In Hobart in 1999, the Pakistanis had Australia on the ropes at 5/126, chasing a total of 369. In just his second Test match, Gilchrist belted 149 not out off 163 balls against one of the best attacks in world cricket, seeing Australia home in one of the highest fourth innings run chases in Test history.

Cricket is a simple game that can become over-complicated by a myriad of theories. By getting Adam to 'just hit the ball' Stan was helping him to unclutter his mind and bat instinctively. As Adam wrote in *True Colours: My Life*, 'When I became an international cricketer and got a name for free hitting, somewhere buried in my subconscious was the sheer delight I'd take when Dad gave me licence to just have a good time and hit the ball.' This backyard training, combined with the fact he was picked as a keeper, not purely as a batsman, allowed him to bat with a sense of freedom seldom seen in cricket's professional age.

Adam Gilchrist was fortunate to be born with talent, drive, competitive older siblings and a very good coach for a father. There's no reason why a boy with similar attributes raised in the same country towns Adam grew up in wouldn't flourish today. Henry Street, Deniliquin, still has expansive front lawns made for playing long games of cricket. Goonellabah still has its fair share of big backyards and open spaces. The Gilchrists' old place still has its backyard net. Maybe it's inspiring other dads in the area to build their own, just as the Gilchrists once were by the backyard net on the Ballina Cutting. But where do you find a mum who will throw you balls these days for hours at a time? In early 2007, I saw a woman chucking cricket balls relentlessly at her twelve-year-old son. The location? Neilson Park in Lismore, 4 kilometres from the Gilchrist home.

Backyard Nets

If you want to become a Test cricketer it helps if your father can pour concrete and put up a fence. While few can match Adam Gilchrist's backyard set-up with its astroturf pitch, bowling machine, video analysis, and qualified live-in coach, Australian cricket owes much to a band of dedicated dads who set up backyard training facilities for their sons.

• • •

Legendary Victorian opening pair Bill Ponsford and Bill Woodfull both had custom-built practice pitches. Woodfull's father Thomas, a Methodist clergyman, had a pitch laid behind the parsonage in Gipps Street, Collingwood. Woodfull was not the only future Test captain to benefit from the reverend's foresight. A young Jack Ryder also practised on the parson's pitch. Ponsford, the only Australian to score two quadruple centuries, trained with his brother Ray on a bitumen pitch in their Elsternwick backyard. The current owners found remnants of the pitch while digging in the garden.

• • •

Justin Langer and Matthew Hayden can also trace their love of occupying the crease to home built nets. Colin Langer installed a concrete pitch in the bottom corner of his Perth backyard and surrounded it with steel netting. Justin and his brothers Adam and Jono weren't allowed to use the pitch until they painted the old man's fence. At the Haydens' peanut farm in Kingaroy, father Laurie levelled out a turf pitch with his tractor grader and surrounded it with a 2-metre high steel mesh fence. Brothers Matt and Gary could train all day without having to spend valuable time chasing the ball. However the nets couldn't do much to stop a booming straight drive from ending up in the corn field across the road.

• • •

At Wondai, around 30 kilometres north of the Haydens' property, another home-made track bore fruit. Bob Rackemann poured a concrete pitch for Carl's fifteenth birthday and fenced it in. Rackemann describes it as 'very helpful' to his development as a fast bowler. Another Queensland quickie, Craig McDermott, bowled at his older brother Mark on a home-made concrete pitch in the family backyard at Ipswich. Part of the back fence was missing and the adjoining block was vacant, so young McDermott could steam in and skid the ball off the concrete at full tilt.

• • •

Slow bowlers have also benefited from their fathers' concrete pouring skills. Australia's most successful off-spinner, Ashley Mallett, bowled for hours at his brother Nick on the family pitch at Morley in Western Australia. Raymond Mallett poured his boys a concrete pitch and surrounded it with chicken wire in an attempt to save the lawn and the back windows from destruction. Leg-spinner Bruce Dooland, who took over a thousand first-class wickets and taught Richie Benaud the flipper, learned his craft on a concrete pitch laid by his father Walter. Left-arm slowie George Tribe practised his spinners on a neighbour's concrete pitch in Yarraville.

• • •

Victorian opener Matthew Elliott faced up to his two younger brothers on a half-sized concrete pitch laid at Kyabram by his father John. Dashing Blayney bat, Peter Toohey, had a concrete pitch with nets built for him by his dad, Alan, when he was around six or seven years old. Every afternoon after school, Peter practised in the nets, either with his brothers or by himself. The four Toohey boys also had football goalposts built for them out the back of the family farm.

• • •

Tasmanian Jack Badcock was another Test cricketer to benefit from the handyman skills of a farming father. Lindsay Badcock not only built his son a concrete pitch, he hand-crafted bats from willow trees growing on the family property. At the time of the Bodyline series they put the pitch to good use. Lindsay threw short-pitched deliveries at Jack in case he got a call up to the Test team. Badcock wasn't required during the Bodyline series, but he made his Test debut against England in 1936. Badcock, like so many Test cricketers, owed a huge debt to his father. When you build your boy a practice pitch it gives them an opportunity to practise in the kind of obsessive manner that's required if you want to make it to the top.

Mike Hussey

PITCH: Concrete driveway in the backyard.

BAT: Started with a hunk of wood, graduated to a regular cricket bat.

BALL: Started with stones, graduated to tennis balls, which were often taped to increase swing.

WICKET: Three stumps placed in the holes of a single brick.

PLAYERS: Mike, David and occasionally Ted, their father.

RULES: Over the fence was out, automatic wicketkeeper, no LBW.

PLAYERS' COMFORT LEVEL: Volatile. Dangerous conditions that could easily descend into violence.

When Mike Hussey first got a taste for cricket, the game was undergoing a revolution. World Series Cricket was changing the way cricket was played, and what players were paid. Test cricket, once dominated by bank tellers, teachers and cigarette salesmen, became a professional sport. One-day cricket with its frenetic hitting, coloured clothes and day-night games found a market for fans lacking the time or patience for five-day cricket.

TV coverage, previously ponderous and one-dimensional, became a slick multi-camera operation. Equipment changed too; helmets protected batsmen from short-pitched bowling; padding became more robust; and bats more hi-tech. Young boys emulated their heroes using Gray-Nicholls bats with scoops carved in the backs. Not that everything new was embraced. Dennis Lillee became an instant expert in the market for scrap metal when sales of his aluminium bat hit freefall.

In the midst of all this progress, Mike Hussey's cricket remained rooted in the Stone Age. While Australian batsmen were getting used to facing chin music produced by an unfriendly West Indian quartet, young Mike was having rocks thrown at him by his Dad. There was no cricket kit in the Hussey household, not even a tennis ball. Mike's first bat was a hunk of sawn-off wood; the 'balls' were pieces of gravel bowled awkwardly by his father.

Ted Hussey was no fan of cricket. While working as a public affairs manager at Australia Post, he was asked to play in the annual cricket game between the Planning Branch and the Building Branch. Ted was an accomplished sprinter and basketballer, but he had no desire to play any form of cricket. This was not good enough for the long-socked bureaucrats at Australia Post. 'At that stage of the game, the threat at the Post Office was if you cut up rough or made a blunder you'd be sent to Wyndham.' Hussey recalls. 'The planning manager appeared at my door and said you've got two choices son, you're playing cricket or you're going to Wyndham.'

Ted decided he'd better get some practice in. Each player had to bowl at least one over, and in the blokey culture of an Australia Post cricket game, any sign of weakness was ripe for some workplace harassment. He handed his three-year-old son Mike a lump of wood and started bowling pieces of gravel at him. While his father's technique was rusty, Mike was a natural. 'The eye was there,' Ted remembers, 'he could seem them clearly, I can still see him hitting them now.'

While Mike's first hit was encouraging, Ted's first game was a disaster. He was out twice within two balls for a duck. The first time, being a social game, didn't count. He did take one wicket, the opposition's star batsmen, caught on the boundary off a ball that bounced twice. His team mates were in hysterics. To top off the day, Ted Hussey was awarded a trophy for 'turning up'. Humiliated, he drove home in a foul mood. 'I thought to myself I will never ever play that bloody game again!' When he arrived home, Mike was waiting for his father, with the lump of wood in hand. His first words to his father as he got out of the car were: 'Dad, will you play cricket with me?'

Soon the pieces of gravel were replaced by tennis balls and the hunk of wood was superseded by a home-made bat. Even Ted's double-bouncing slow balls became redundant. David, two years Mike's junior, became the cannon fodder for his brother's long innings in the backyard. Mike was already obsessed by cricket. That gave David the advantage he needed. He could always tell his older brother he wouldn't play unless he got to bat first. These games were played with an intensity that was probably only matched in the Chappell and Waugh backyards. Younger sisters Kate and Gemma were too sensible to get involved. These were one-on-one grudge matches played to the death. 'Dave was never out,' Mike wrote in *Mr Cricket*. 'If he nicked one to the keeper, he wouldn't walk. Even if he got clean bowled he refused to hand over the bat! It was then that the fights would start.'

The Hussey boys would not have been in the running for any 'spirit of cricket' awards, if such things existed back then. There was not only cheating going on in their backyard games, but regular punch-ups followed disputed decisions. The two boys used the pace they'd inherited from their father to chase each other around the backyard when dismissals weren't accepted. When things got really bad David would lock himself in the car and refuse to come out. 'That's how so many of our games ended,' Mike wrote. 'Him in tears running away from me and me crying because I'd been hoodwinked again into bowling for ages and not getting to bat.'

When Mike did eventually get a bat he had to work hard to make sure Dave didn't take his wicket. The Hussey pitch was a concrete driveway that swung round the back of the house into a carport. The bowler could make the ball deviate sharply by hitting the grooves in between the concrete slabs that were perfectly in line with middle stump. Mike knew he had to make the most of each innings and make sure he didn't get out. Otherwise Dave's reluctance to leave the wicket would condemn him to spending his afternoon bowling under the hot West Australian sun. In the backyard at Mullaloo, survival became the cornerstone of his batting.

Ted Hussey believes these early contests were critical to the development of his two boys and their individual styles that led them to representing Australia. 'It was the competition between the two of them that developed their different types of game. All Dave wants to do is beat you and the mind is ticking over all the time of how the hell he's going to get you. That's what happened in the backyard. He wanted to beat Mike. The other fella [Mike] will stay there and stay there and he'll wait till you make a mistake.'

When Mike first started playing organised cricket for Whitfords Cricket Club in the under 12s, there wasn't much power to his batting. Like Keith Miller, he was a small boy in his youth, and had to base his game around defence. Bob Mitchell, his first coach, taught him to concentrate on technique and survival. It was an attitude reinforced by his father Ted. 'Get your technique right and fight hard, I would always tell the two boys, and the rest will follow.'

For a non-cricketer, Ted Hussey had a huge influence on the cricket careers of his sons. He applied what he learned from athletics to cricket. By the time they turned four, he'd taught his boys how to run with the correct posture. Balance and footwork is critical when it comes to batting. As Ted puts it, 'If you run a lot, you will find that your feet will start to work on the crease.'

Ted also knew how to give his sons an edge in physical fitness and mental toughness. The boys swam at the beach and ran in the sand hills. Pre-season training meant Sunday morning runs through the soft sand at a time most of their peers were probably sleeping off the previous night. The boys pumped iron in a pre-historic gym where the weights were old and rusty and the environment was cold and damp. Ted believed in what he called 'accelerating the implement' – the repetitive use of light weights to help mimic the quick movements needed to play shots against a fast-moving ball.

Cricket in the late 1970s and early 1980s provided plenty of captivating contests for young cricket fans to watch on the television. Clive Lloyd's dominant West Indies side seemed to be out here every second summer. The Australian team was full of characters that played combative cricket. Mike's favourites were Allan Border, Dennis Lillee and Rod Marsh. Border's string of gutsy innings against the fearsome attacks of the Windies must've had a huge influence on young Mike. In photos as a youngster, he's seen batting right-handed. But he shifted to left-handed so he could be more like AB. Even now, his defiant style and the way he bats with the tail, evokes the spirit of his childhood hero.

As with most cricketers born in the 1970s, Mike was a beneficiary of another cricket revolution. In 1979 in Perth, indoor cricket started in Australia. By 1984, there were around 200,000 registered players. For cricket nuts like Mike Hussey it meant indoor nets were available all year, all day and all night, no matter what the weather was like. Mike used to work on his batting at the indoor nets three or four nights a week with his coach Ian Kevan. Mike was facing around a 1000 balls a week – the equivalent of every ball bowled in a Test match over two days. On one occasion when his club side had a bye, Mike took it as an opportunity to have a six-hour, one-on-one training session. The day was split into three two-hour sessions, just like a Test match. 'During one of the breaks I actually fell asleep because I was buggered,' Kevan recalled in *Mr Cricket*. 'When I woke up I asked one of the fellas nearby where Michael had gone and he said, "He's just gone for a run," I couldn't believe it.'

While the enclosed spaces of the local indoor cricket centre became the perfect environment for Mike's obsessive training methods, it was the wide open spaces of Mullaloo that provided those crucial first opportunities for the Hussey boys. When Ted and Helen Hussey moved to Mullaloo in 1973 it was one of the fringe suburbs of Perth. All the houses were on big blocks and there was plenty of open space for kids to run around in. While the local indoor centre is still there, the backyards of Mullaloo are evaporating. The old quarter-acre blocks are being subdivided, with two houses being built to a block. The Husseys' old backyard has not been battle-axed. There's still plenty of room to play cricket, though Ted Hussey has built a shed on part of where the old pitch used to be. No doubt it's a more tranquil environment now than it was when his boys were playing their cut-throat Test matches in the 1980s.

Brett Lee

PITCH: Concrete driveway.

BAT: Normal bat.

BALL: Tennis ball (sometimes taped), or cricket ball when parents were out.

STUMPS: Garbage bin.

PLAYERS: Brett and his brothers Shane and Grant.

RULES: Over the fence six and out (except straight down the ground), off-side fence on the full out. Automatic wicket-keeper.

HAZARDS: Joins in concrete pitch made the ball dart and jag.

BACKYARD DRILLS: Spin and pace throw downs off the paving.

PLAYERS' COMFORT LEVEL: Particularly tough on Brett and Grant, who had to bowl uphill to an older brother who was a good bat and a non-walker.

If you take a look up the driveway at 8 Winter Avenue, Mt Warrigal, you get some understanding why Brett Lee became a fast bowler. The concrete strip, which was the pitch for the Lee brothers' backyard Tests, is around 30 metres long. There are no run-up constraints here. If you open up the driveway gate and cross the road, as Brett used to do, you can charge in from an even greater distance. As the younger brother of a punishing batsman, Brett got plenty of practice coming in off the long run.

Five years separated the Lee brothers. Shane was three years older than Brett; Grant was two years younger again. The pecking order was straightforward. Shane batted first, Brett bowled, Grant fielded. Brett got used to toiling away in the searing heat of summer. 'I got 400 one day,' Shane recalls. 'I think I was out a couple of times, but being the older brother I didn't take it. Brett got to bat after bowling to me for at least three hours, and I knocked him over first ball. I went inside and he started to cry, and Mum gave me a smack and sent me out to bowl at him again. But I think he only got 11 second dig.' When Brett played cricket against boys his own age it must've seemed so much simpler. In his first competition game for the Oak Flats Rats under 10s, he took 6/0 in his first over.

The driveway pitch wasn't always conducive to quadruple centuries. While you did have to bowl uphill, there was plenty of bounce off the concrete and some sideways movement as well. Adam Gilchrist made a guest appearance on the driveway pitch when he and Shane were playing together for New South Wales. 'They're nasty conditions, with cracks in the driveway." Gilchrist recalls.

The cracks were where the slabs of cement were joined. If the ball hit these, it could either take off, or shoot along the ground.

The Tests were played as three-way games, two innings per side. Shane was Australia; Brett the West Indies; Grant, being the youngest, had to put up with being England. The boys used a bin for a wicket and the garage door acted as automatic wicketkeeper. The house is no longer owned by the Lees, but evidence remains of their games. The garage door resembles a hail-damaged car. While the brothers played mostly with a tennis ball, the hard ball came out when Mum and Dad weren't around. Some of the dents on the roller door are quite high, which shows you how many throat balls were being bowled. Bob Lee had already replaced one roller door before the current one was installed. 'It got to the stage it was that tattered from balls hitting it, it wouldn't even go up,' Shane recalls. 'You couldn't lock the garage to go out.'

The garage door was not the only thing to cop a beating. The light next to the letterbox was constantly getting smashed. After one too many cover drives the wooden fence on the off side of the pitch fell down and had to be replaced. Veronica Zdraveski, who lived next door for 14 years, says she's amazed none of her windows were ever broken. But one of the backyard rules stated that if you hit the fence on the full on the off-side it was automatically out. This meant the boys kept the ball along the ground through cover and point. This rule not only saved the neighbours' windows, it had a lasting impact on both Brett and Shane's batting. The cut shot has never been a favourite stroke of either cricketer. With the fence just metres away it was impossible to cut without hitting the fence on the full.

The main scoring opportunities were at square leg, where there was a gap between the garage and the house, and straight down the ground. Once again this had an influence on the Lee boys' batting in later years. Shane's first boundary in international cricket was a clip off the toes from a Courtney Walsh delivery. 'I was always very good off my pads,' Shane recalls, 'and now thinking about it, it was probably one of the main reasons.'

While over the fence was 'six and out', over the fence behind the bowler's head was six, but you were able to bat on. This encouraged straight hitting. Clearing the neighbour's roof on the opposite side of the road became the ultimate mark of fine batsmanship. Both Brett and Shane favoured hitting straight down the ground later in their careers.

Few tailenders play the short ball better than Brett Lee. During the Ashes series in 2005, he was consistently hit by England's four fast men, but he held his ground and scored runs in vital partnerships. On the concrete driveway at Mt Warrigal his elder brother provided him with a good initiation to the short ball. 'I'd always pad him up with all the gear we had, and a helmet and bounce the hell out of him,' laughs Shane. 'I was a bit sadistic.'

While Richie Benaud and the Chappell brothers wrote down their backyard Test results in scorebooks, the Lee boys had more high-tech accounting methods. In 1982, the Commodore 64 personal computer was launched. The C64 did for home computers what the Model T Ford did for cars. It was the first affordable PC and sold around 30 million units worldwide. Its American designers probably didn't anticipate it would be used in Australia to collate statistics for backyard cricket matches, but that's exactly what the Lee brothers used it for. They were able to work out their aggregates and averages and compare them to the Test players they'd been watching on television.

The boys supplemented their backyard games with training sessions down at the nets opposite their local primary school. Their father Bob worked as a metallurgist at the BHP steelworks. He finished work at 3 pm and took the boys to the nets two or three times a week. It helped his sons improve their cricket and gave the garage door some relief. While Bob Lee was no cricketer of note, he and their uncle Les bowled at the boys and encouraged them to keep practising. Bob also helped them with the mental side of the game, teaching them the importance of finishing off your opponents when you're on top.

The Lee brothers also did specific batting drills on the paved area of the backyard. If one of them was due to face a good quick bowler on the weekend they padded up and faced some rising deliveries thrown from short range. These sessions helped tune the reflexes and decision-making processes, allowing them to work out whether to duck, defend or attack. This was not unlike the drill the Harvey brothers practised with a marble off the concrete in their backyard. If an opposition team contained a good spinner, the Lee boys practised facing flighted, turning deliveries off the paving.

The constant backyard games and net sessions paid off. All three Lee boys played for New South Wales under 17s. Shane went on to play 45 one-day internationals for Australia. Brett became the fourth Australian to take 300 Test wickets. Grant, who displayed the same kind of potential as his brothers, retired at the age of 18 when he found he wasn't enjoying the game.

Shane Lee is adamant that the backyard games played a major role in both him and Brett playing for Australia. 'I've thought about this a lot. I think players now should train more like you do in the backyard. That is, hitting a huge amount of balls and bowling a huge amount. If you're batting and you're facing 1000 tennis balls every week, often when you get to state level you get two or three net sessions a week and you're only batting for seven minutes, you're not facing anywhere near that many balls. It really honed your skills and got your reflexes up and made it a lot easier to play when you got out in the middle.'

There's nothing to stop a bunch of talented brothers in Mt Warrigal today from practising like the Lees. The conditions at 8 Winter Avenue haven't changed much. Even that battered garage door remains. Mt Warrigal and the other surrounding suburbs on the shores of Lake Illawarra retain a country feel. There's plenty of open space and a lack of the kind of McMansions that have come to dominate the capital cities. Cricket is still played by young boys in the neighbourhood. The Oak Flats Rats have got enough players to make up six junior teams. But Veronica Zdraveski doesn't hear the thud of ball on garage door anymore. The Lees' former neighbour says she doesn't see or hear any evidence of backyard cricket being played in Winter Avenue.

Acknowledgements

This book started as a conversation at a suburban cricket ground in Sydney. Each summer for seventeen seasons I spent my Saturdays playing cricket for the Lindfield District Cricket Club. The banter was as much fun as the cricket itself. When batting, we'd drag half a dozen well-worn couches out of the clubhouse, plonk them in the grandstand and watch our team mates take on the opposition bowlers. As we watched, we talked, and over many seasons no topic, no question, no argument, no piece of character asssasination was off-limits.

One Saturday we started picking apart the technique of our number 3 batsmen Rob Wynn Jones. A bespectacled, combativite lawyer with a talent for riling opposition players, Rob had a hook shot to match his mouth. It was unorthodox, but effective, played like a paddle shot around the corner between the keeper and deep fine leg. It infuriated fast bowlers and got us talking.

'Where the hell did you learn to play that shot?' one of us asked. 'In the backyard,' Rob replied, 'On the leg side of my backyard pitch were windows, from mid-on to square-leg. If I hit them I was out. So I had to play my hook shot around the corner, just past the keeper.' As the conversation bounced around the team, everyone had a similar story of a strength or weakness that could be attributed to their backyard.

It got me thinking; surely it must be the same for elite cricketers. The tales from their backyard games must tell a broader story of how they made it as Test cricketers. Sure enough they did. I did a series for ABC Radio on the topic, and that series evolved into this book. So I owe a huge debt of gratitude to my former team mates. Thanks for letting me steal that conversation and turn it into something bigger.

Of course, turning an interview-based radio series into a book was not easy, not for me anyway. I'd never written much beyond the occasional 1000 word piece. I needed to do a lot more research and work out how you actually go about writing a book. So I did the sensible thing. I contacted Gideon Haigh. Gideon deserves special thanks. Not only is he the best cricket writer in the world, he's also exceedingly tolerant when it comes to answering moronic questions about cricket and writing. All those seasons doing Chris Tavaré impersonations for the Yarras have obviously taught him patience.

A big thanks to all the players, and their relatives and friends, who spoke to me for this book. It was joy to talk to them and see their eyes light up as they recalled their backyard Test matches. I hope today's generation of kids will one day be able to remember their childhood games with as much pleasure.

The following friends and colleagues helped with suggestions, contacts, feedback, book loans, spare beds and sound advice: John Joyce, Lyn Haultain, Francis Leach, Adam Spencer, David Sygall, Melinda Lyons, Luke Foley, Guy Mankey, Rodney Cavalier and Ed Wright. Ed deserves a special mention for his editing skills, his ideas and for insisting that Phil Collins references, even dererogatory ones, have no place in a credible book about cricket.

Thanks to Jody Lee at ABC Books for getting the idea up, having patience while I worked out how and when I was going to write the book, and for understanding that most reporters have a natural instinct to not do what they're told. Linda Brainwood did a fantastic job sourcing the pictures. Thanks to Richie

Benaud, Greg Chappell, Ted Hussey, Vic Grimmett, Shane Lee, Peter O'Reilly and Doug Walters who allowed me to reproduce the photos from their family albums.

I've spent a lot of time in libraries over the last couple of years, scouring collections looking for stories about backyard cricket. A big thanks to all those who helped me out especially David Studham and the staff at the Melbourne Cricket Club Library and Dr Colin Clowes at the NSW Cricket Association Library. I wrote and researched much of this book at the Mitchell Library in Sydney, one of the finest public institutions in Australia, a place where school kids, scholars, researchers and the homeless share tables and get lost in books.

The biggest thanks of all goes to Elise, my wife. Elise doesn't like cricket. She once fell asleep in prime seats, behind the bowler's arm, in the first session of the first day of a Sydney Test. But she has graciously tolerated my obsession with a game that takes a hell of a long time to play and watch. Not only has she put up with me ruining her weekends by playing cricket for countless years, she's now put up with me ruining her weekends writing about it. Thanks for all your support. I wouldn't have been able to write this book, or do anything else of much note, without you.

Bibliography

Books

Allen, Peter, *Farewell to Bradman*, Macmillan, Sydney, 2001

Barker, Ralph, *Ten Great Bowlers*, Chatto & Windus, London, 1967

Bailey, Trevor and Trueman, Fred, *From Larwood to Lillee*, Queen Anne Press, London, 1983

Barnes, Sid, *It Isn't Cricket*, Collins, London, 1953

Baum, Greg, *The Waugh Era*, ABC Books, Sydney, 2004

Beldam, George W. and Fry, C.B., *Great Batsmen: Their Methods at a Glance*, Macmillan & Co., London, 1905

Benaud, John, *Matters of Choice*, Swan Publishing, Western Australia, 1997

Benaud, Lou, *The Young Cricketer*, Angus & Robertson, Sydney, 1964

Benaud, Richie, *Anything But . . . an Autobiography*, Hodder & Stoughton, London, 1998

Benaud, Richie, *My Spin on Cricket*, Hodder & Stoughton, London, 2005

Benaud, Richie, *On Reflection*, Collins, Sydney, 1984

Benaud, Richie, *Willow Patterns*, Hodder & Stoughton, London, 1969

Border, Allan, *Allan Border: An Autobiography*, Methuen, Sydney, 1986

Border, Allan, *Beyond Ten Thousand: My Life Story*, Swan Publishing, London, 1993

Bradman, Don, *Farewell to Cricket*, Hodder & Stoughton, London, 1950

Bradman, Sir Donald *The Art of Cricket*, Hodder & Stoughton, London, 1958

Brayshaw, Ian, *Caught Marsh Bowled Lillee: The Legend Lives On*, ABC Books, Sydney, 2001

Browning, Mark, *Richie Benaud: Cricketer, Captain, Guru*, Kangaroo Press, Sydney, 1996

Cardwell, Ronald, *The Fitzroy Urchin*, Cherrybrook, 1999

Cashman, Richard (ed.) et al., *The Oxford Companion to Australian Cricket*, Oxford University Press, Sydney, 1996

Cashman, Richard and Weaver, Amanda, *Wicket Women: Cricket and Women in Australia*, NSW University Press, Sydney, 1991

Chappell, Greg, *Cricket: The Making of Champions*, Lothian Books, Melbourne, 2004

Chappell, Ian, *Chappelli: Ian Chappell's Life Story*, Hutchinson, London, 1976

Chappell, Ian, *Chappelli: The Cutting Edge*, Swan Publishing, Western Australia, 1992

Craddock, Robert, *The Ian Healy Story: Playing For Keeps*, Swan Publishing, Western Australia, 1996

Cutten History Committee of the Fitzroy History Society, *Fitzroy: Melbourne's First Suburb*, Hyland House, Flemington, Victoria, 1989

Davidson, Alan, *Fifteen Paces*, Marlin Books, Richmond, Victoria, 1977

Derriman, Philip (ed.) *Our Don Bradman*, ABC Books, Sydney, 2001

Derriman, Philip, *The Best of Keepers: The Life and Artistry of Don Tallon*, Cricket Publishing, 2000

Egan, Jack, *One Who Will: The Search for Steve Waugh*, Allen & Unwin, Sydney, 2004

Fiddian, Marc, *Ponsford & Woodfull, A Premier Partnership*, Five Mile Press, Fitzroy, Victoria, 1988

Fiddian, Marc, *A Life-long Innings: The Jack Ryder Story*, Packenham Gazette, 1995

Fingleton, Jack, *Fingleton on Cricket*, Collins, London, 1972

Fingleton, Jack, *Masters of Cricket: From Trumper to May*, Heinemann, London, 1958

Fingleton, Jack, *The Immortal Victor Trumper*, Collins, London, 1978

Fitzgerald, Shirley, *Rising Damp: Sydney 1870–90*, Oxford University Press, Sydney, 1987

FitzSimons, Peter, *Steve Waugh*, HarperCollins Publishers, Sydney, 2004

Frith, David, *The Fast Men*, Van Nostrand Reinhold, Berkshire, 1975

Frith, David, *The Slow Men*, Horwitz Grahame with Richard Smart Publishing, Sydney, 1984

Gately, Mark, *Waugh Declared: The Story of Australia's Famous Cricketing Twins*, Ironbark Press, Sydney, 1992

Gilchrist, Adam, *True Colours: My Life*, Pan Macmillan, Sydney, 2008

Gladwell, Malcolm, *Outliers: The Story of Success*, Allen Lane, London, 2008

Haigh, Gideon, *One Summer, Every Summer: An Ashes Journal*, Text Publishing, Melbourne, 1995

Haigh, Gideon, *The Green and Golden Age*, Black Inc, Melbourne, 2007

Haigh, Gideon, *The Summer Game*, Text Publishing, Melbourne, 1997

Harvey, Neil, *My World of Cricket*, Hodder & Stoughton, London, 1963

Healy, Ian, *Hands and Heals: The Autobiography*, HarperCollins Publishers, Sydney, 2000

Hibbins, G.M., *A Short History of Collingwood*, Collingwood Historical Society, 1997

Hussey, Michael and Sygall, David, *Mr Cricket: Driven to Succeed*, Hardie Grant, Melbourne, 2007

James, Alfred, *The Don Versus the Rest: The Scorecards of the Minor Cricket Matches Played by Sir Donald Bradman, 1920/21 to 1962/63*, ABM James, Wahroonga, 2006

Keating, Christopher, *Surry Hills*, Hale & Iremonger, Sydney, 1991

Knight, James, *Lee to the Power of Two*, HarperCollins Publishers, Sydney, 2001

Knight, James, *Mark Waugh: The Biography*, HarperCollins Publishers, Sydney, 2003

Langer, Justin, *The Power of Passion*, Swan Sport, Western Australia, 2002

Lecky, John, *Records Are Made to Be Broken: The Real Story of Bill Ponsford*, Arcadia, 2006

Lillee, Dennis, *The Art of Fast Bowling*, Collins, Sydney, 1977

Lillee, Dennis and Brayshaw, Ian, *Back to the Mark*, Hutchinson, Melbourne, 1974

Lillee, Dennis, *Menace*, Headline, Sydney, 2003

Lillee, Dennis, *My Life in Cricket*, Methuen, North Ryde, 1982

Lindwall, Ray, *Flying Stumps*, Arrow, London, 1954

Macartney, C.G., *My Cricketing Days*, William Heinemann, London, 1930

McCool, Colin, *Cricket is a Game*, Stanley Paul, London, 1961

McDermott, Craig, *McDermott: Strike Bowler*, ABC Books, Sydney, 1992

McGrath, Glenn and Lane, Daniel, *Line and Strength*, William Heinemann, Sydney, 2008

McGrath, Glenn and Lane, Daniel, *Pacemaker: The Inner Thoughts of Glenn McGrath*, Ironbark, Sydney, 1998

McGregor, Adrian, *Greg Chappell: Cricket's Incomparable Artist*, University of Queensland Press, St Lucia, 1990

McHarg, Jack, *Bill O'Reilly: A Cricketing Life*, Millennium, Newtown, 1990

McHarg, Jack, *Lindsay Hassett: One of a Kind*, Simon and Schuster, Sydney, 1998

McHarg, Jack, *Stan McCabe: The Man and his Cricket*, Collins, Sydney, 1987

Mackinolty, Judy (ed.), *The Wasted Years? Australia's Great Depression*, Allen & Unwin, Sydney, 1981

Mailey, Arthur, *10 for 66 and All That*, Phoenix Sports Books, London, 1958

Mallett, Ashley, *Bradman's Band*, University of Queensland Press, St Lucia, 2000

Mallett, Ashley and Chappell, Ian, *Chappelli Speaks Out*, Allen & Unwin, Sydney, 2007

Mallett, Ashley, *Clarrie Grimmet: The Bradman of Spin*, University of Queensland Press, St Lucia, 1993

Mallett, Ashley, *Dennis Lillee*, Hutchinson, Richmond, 1982

Mallett, Ashley, *Doug Walters*, Hutchinson, Richmond, 1982

Mallett, Ashley, *Kim Hughes*, Hutchinson, Richmond, 1984

Mallett, Ashley, *One of a Kind: The Doug Walters Story*, Allen & Unwin, Sydney, 2008

Mallett, Ashley, *The Chappell Brothers*, Hutchinson, Richmond, 1982

Mallett, Ashley, *Trumper: The Illustrated Biography*, Macmillan, Sydney, 1985

Martin-Jenkins, Christopher, *The Spirit of Cricket: A Personal Anthology*, Faber & Faber, London, 1994

Meher-Homji, Kersi, *The Waugh Twins: The Cricketing Story of Steve Waugh and Mark Waugh*, Kangaroo Press, Sydney, 1998

Miller, Keith, *Cricket Crossfire*, Oldbourne Press, London, 1956

Moyes, A.G. ('Johnnie'), *Benaud*, Angus & Robertson, Sydney, 1962

Murray, James, *Larrikins*, Lansdowne Press, Sydney, 1973

Noble, M.A., *The Game's the Thing*, Cassell & Co, London, 1926

O'Reilly, Bill, *Tiger: 60 Years of Cricket*, Collins, Sydney, 1985

Page, Michael, *Bradman*, Macmillan, Sydney, 1988

Piesse, Ken and Wilson, Alf, *Bradmans of the Bush: The Legends and Larrikins of Australian Bush Cricket*, Penguin Books, Melbourne, 2003

Pickett, Charles, *The Fibro Frontier: A Different History of Australian Architecture*, Powerhouse Publishing, Sydney, 1997

Perry, Roland, *Bradman's Best Ashes Teams: Sir Donald Bradman's Selection of the Best Ashes Teams in Cricket History*, Random House, Sydney, 2002

Perry, Roland, *Miller's Luck*, Random House, Sydney, 2005

Perry, Roland, *The Don*, Macmillan, Sydney, 1995

Perry, Roland, *Waugh's Way: The Steve Waugh Story: Learner, Legend, Leader*, Random House, Sydney, 2002

Pollard, Jack (ed.), *After Stumps Were Drawn: The Best of Ray Robinson's Cricket Writing*, William Collins, Sydney, 1985

Pollard, Jack, *Australian Cricket: The Game and the Players*, Hodder & Stoughton Australia in association with Australian Broadcasting Commission, Sydney, 1982

Pollard, Jack (ed.), *Cricket, the Australian Way*, Lansdowne, Sydney, 1968

Pollard, Jack, *Six and Out: The Legend of Australian and New Zealand Cricket*, Pollard Publishing, Sydney, 1970

Pollard, Jack, *Six and Out* (enlarged 6th edn), Pollard Publishing, Sydney, 1980

Raiji Vasant (ed.), *Victor Trumper: The Beau Ideal of a Cricketer*, Vivek Publications, India, 1964

Redpath, Ian and Phillipson, Neil, *Always Reddy*, Garry Sparke & Associates, Toorak, 1976

Reese, Daniel, *Was It All Cricket?*, George Allen & Unwin, London, 1948

Richardson, V.Y and Whitington, R.S., *The Vic Richardson Story: The Autobiography of a Versatile Sportsman*, Rigby, Adelaide, 1967

Ringwood, John, *Ray Lindwall: Cricket Legend*, Kangaroo Press, Sydney, 1995

Robinson, Ray and Haigh, Gideon, *On Top Down Under: Australia's Cricket Captains*, Wakefield Press, Adelaide, 1996

Rosenwater, Irving, *Sir Donald Bradman*, Anchor Press, London, 1978

Sharpham, Peter, *Charlie Macartney: Cricket's 'Governor General'*, Walla Walla Press, Petersham, 2004

Sharpham, Peter, *Trumper: The Definitive Biography*, Hodder & Stoughton, Sydney, 1985

Shillinglaw, A.L. and Hale, Brian, *Bradman Revisited*, The Parrs Wood Press, Manchester, 2003

Simpson, Bobby, *Captain's Story*, Stanley Paul & Co, London, 1966

Simpson, Bob, *Simmo: Cricket Then and Now*, Allen & Unwin, Sydney, 2006

Smith, Rick, *Cricket's Enigma: The Sid Barnes Story*, ABC Books, Sydney, 1999

Walters, Doug and Laws, Ken, *The Doug Walters Story*, Rigby, Adelaide, 1981

Walters, Doug and Waugh, Mark, *The Entertainers, Talking Cricket Then and Now*, Random House, Sydney, 1999

Waters, Ken, *Champions by Chance and by Choice*, K. and C. Waters, Western Australia, 2006

Waugh, Steve, *Out of My Comfort Zone: The Autobiography*, Viking, Melbourne, 2005

Whitington, R.S., *Keith Miller: The Golden Nugget*, Rigby, Adelaide, 1981

Whitington, R.S., *Time of the Tiger: The Bill O'Reilly Story*, Hutchinson, Sydney, 1970

National Library of Australia Oral History Collection

Belinda Clark: interviewed by Nikki Henningham, 2008

Neil Harvey: interviewed by Neil Bennetts, 1980

Ray Lindwall: interviewed by John Ringwood, 1990

Keith Miller: interviewed by Neil Bennetts, 1981

Bill O'Reilly: interviewed by John Ringwood, 1992

Betty Wilson: interviewed by Nikki Hennigham, 2007

Broadcast media

Bradman: The Don Declares, ABC Radio, 1987

Bradman, Australian Broadcasting Corporation ABC Video 1991

Cricket in the 70s: The Chappell Era, ABC TV

Enough Rope, ABC TV

7.30 Report, ABC TV

That's Cricket, 1931

The Kid Stakes, 1927

Print media

The Australian, *Inside Sport*, *Sport Health*, *The Sydney Morning Herald*, *The Weekend Australian*, *Wisden*, *Wisden Cricketers' Almanack*

Online

www.adamgilchrist.com

www.austmus.gov.au

www.cricinfo.com

Author interviews

Troy Arnold

Jan Beames

John Benaud

Richie Benaud

Johnno Border

Greg Chappell

Ian Chappell

Belinda Clark

Colin Clark

Alan Davidson

Brian Gainsford

Adam Gilchrist

Stan Gilchrist

Jason Gillespie

Vic Grimmett

Brett Hanson

Neil Harvey

Laurie Hayden

Greg Healy

Ian Healy

Mike Hussey

Ted Hussey

Moises Henriques

Graham King

Geoff Lawson

Shane Lee

Chris McLeod

Marc McMahon

Ashley Mallett

Colin Miller

Peter O'Reilly

Carl Rackemann

Warren Saunders

Bob Simpson

Keith Stackpole

George Tribe

Peter Toohey

Ken Waters

Doug Walters

Norma Ward

Betty Wilson

George Wilson

Veronica Zdraveski

First Tests Statistics

Victor Trumper

Tests	Inns	NO	Runs	HS	Ave
48	89	8	3163	214*	39.04

Charlie Macartney

Tests	Inns	NO	Runs	HS	Ave
35	55	4	2131	170	41.78

Wkts	Runs	BB	Ave
45	1240	7/58	27.55

Arthur Mailey

Tests	Wkts	Runs	BB	Ave
21	99	3358	9/121	33.91

Clarrie Grimmett

Tests	Wkts	Runs	BB	Ave
37	216	5231	7/40	24.21

Bill O'Reilly

Tests	Wkts	Runs	BB	Ave
27	144	3254	7/54	22.59

Don Bradman

Tests	Inns	NO	Runs	HS	Ave
52	80	10	6996	334	99.94

Sid Barnes

Tests	Inns	NO	Runs	HS	Ave
13	19	2	1072	234	63.05

Keith Miller

Batting

Tests	Inns	NO	Runs	HS	Ave
55	87	7	2958	147	36.97

Bowling

Wkts	Runs	BB	Ave
170	3906	7/60	22.97

Ray Lindwall

Batting

Tests	Inns	NO	Runs	HS	Ave
61	84	13	1502	118	21.15

Bowling

Wkts	Runs	BB	Ave
228	5251	7/38	23.03

Betty Wilson

Batting

Tests	Inns	NO	Runs	HS	Ave
11	16	1	862	127	57.46

Bowling

Wkts	Runs	BB	Ave
68	803	7/7	11.80

Neil Harvey

Tests	Inns	NO	Runs	HS	Ave
79	137	10	6149	205	48.41

Alan Davidson

Batting

Tests	Inns	NO	Runs	HS	Ave
44	61	7	1328	80	24.59

Bowling

Wkts	Runs	BB	Ave
186	3819	7/93	20.53

Richie Benaud

Batting

Tests	Inns	NO	Runs	HS	Ave
63	97	7	2201	122	24.45

Bowling

Wkts	Runs	BB	Ave
248	6704	7/72	27.03

Bob Simpson

Tests	Inns	NO	Runs	HS	Ave
62	111	7	4869	311	46.81

THE CHAPPELL BROTHERS
Ian Chappell

Tests	Inns	NO	Runs	HS	Ave
75	136	10	5345	196	42.42

Greg Chappell

Tests	Inns	NO	Run	HS	Ave
87	151	19	7110	247*	53.86

Trevor Chappell

Tests	Inns	NO	Runs	HS	Ave
3	6	1	79	27	15.80

Doug Walters

Tests	Inns	NO	Runs	HS	Ave
74	125	14	5357	250	48.26

Dennis Lillee

Tests	Wkts	Runs	BB	Ave
70	355	8493	7/83	23.92

Allan Border

Tests	Inns	NO	Runs	HS	Ave
156	265	44	11174	205	50.56

Ian Healy

Tests	Inns	NO	Runs	HS	Ave	Ct	St
119	182	23	4356	161*	27.39	366	29

THE WAUGH BROTHERS

Steve Waugh

Batting

Tests	Inns	NO	Runs	HS	Ave
168	260	46	10927	200	51.06

Bowling

Wkts	Runs	BB	Ave
92	3445	5/28	37.44

Mark Waugh

Batting

Tests	Inns	NO	Runs	HS	Ave
128	209	17	8029	153*	41.81

Bowling

Wkts	Runs	BB	Ave
59	2429	5/40	41.16

Belinda Clark

Tests	Inns	NO	Runs	HS	Ave
15	25	5	919	136	45.95

Glenn McGrath

Tests	Wkts	Runs	BB	Ave
124	563	12186	8/24	21.64

Adam Gilchrist

Tests	Inns	NO	Runs	HS	Ave	Ct	St
96	137	20	5570	204*	47.60	379	37

Mike Hussey (up to April 2010)

Tests	Inns	NO	Runs	HS	Ave
50	86	11	3912	182	52.16

Brett Lee

Tests	Wkts	Runs	BB	Ave
76	310	9554	5/30	30.81

Picture Credits

COVER State Library of Victoria 'Neil Harvey batting with some local boys in the laneway next to his family home' ca. 1948-1955, H2004.100/1686;

p.10   Victor Trumper, National Library of Australia, nla.pic-an23505835;

p.12   from *Cricket The Australian Way*, ed. Jack Pollard, Lansdowne Press, Melbourne, 1962.;

p.19   from *My Cricketing Days* by C.G. Macartney, William Heinemann Ltd, London, 1930;

p 27   from *Cricket The Australian Way*, ed. Jack Pollard, Lansdowne Press, Melbourne, 1962.;

p.33   With the kind permission of Vic Grimmett;

p.40   Joe the fox terrier. With the kind permission of Vic Grimmett;

p.42   from *Cricket The Australian Way*, ed. Jack Pollard, Lansdowne Press, Melbourne, 1962;

p.50   Bill O'Reilly's house at Wingello. With the kind permission of Peter O'Reilly

p.51   from *Images of Bradman* by Peter Allen, James Kemsley, Allen & Kemsley Publishing Pty Ltd, Welby, 1994;

p.62   State Library of Victoria, The Childrens Playground 1935, ref: mp010471;

p.64   Newspix;

p.74   Newspix;

p.81   Newspix;

p.87   Newspix;

p.92   State Library of Victoria, ref: an017821;

p.100   Charles Moses during a 'synthetic' cricket Test radio broadcast in 1934. Sounds of play were produced by striking wooden blocks with the point of a pencil. Newspix;

p.102 from *Fifteen Paces*, by Alan Davidson, Souvenir Press, London, 1963;

p.108   With the kind permission of the Benaud family;

p.116 from *Simmo: Cricket Then and Now*, Allen & Unwin, Crows Nest, 2006;

p.122 Young Greg Chappell at age 8. Newspix;

p.124 The young Chappells – Trevor, Ian and Greg with their father Martin. Newspix;

p.134 Doug on the antbed pitch. With the kind permission of Doug Walters;

p.135 The Walters' family backyard dunny. With the kind permission of Doug Walters;

p.142 Newspix / Michael Potter;

p.148 Allan Border (on right) with his brother John. Newspix;

p.158 26 November 2006. Brisbane QLD. First Test, Day Four, Ashes Tour. Australia vs England at the Gabba. Sun lovers at Southbank Beach, Brisbane watch day four of the Ashes cricket series on the big screen. Newspix / Tony Phillips;

p.160 Newspix;

p.167 Newspix;

p.174 Newspix / Rob McKell;

p.181 Newspix;

p.188 Newspix;

p.198 With the kind permission of the Hussey family;

p.204 With the kind permission of the Lee family;

The author and publisher has made every effort to contact copyright holders, and would be pleased to hear from any copyright holder to correct or insert any omission.